In the Shadow of Mahatma Gandhi

Joan Court

SELENE PRESS

Published by Selene Press
74 Sturton Street
Cambridge
CB1 2QA
Tel: 01223 311828

ISBN 0-9543452-0-7

Cover design by Danuta Mayer

Printed by Elitian Ltd, 112 Mill Road, Cambridge CB1 2BD

PREFACE

Everyone has at least one good book to write, usually an autobiography. Every life is interesting.

Joan Court's life is not just interesting, it is quite amazing.

I have never before come across such an explicit account of such an awful childhood. An alcoholic mother, a father who commits suicide, grandparents who do their duty in part and coolly, an equally unhappy brother, random schooling, erratic feeding…It is a wonder that Joan did not spend most of her adult life in an institution. That her childhood wounded her in many ways is clear enough. She went on to seek the affection which she was not given as a child. Only animals gave that affection back to her in full and undemanding measure.

Yet despite all this, it is a triumphant story which gripped me from start to finish. My heart warmed to the description of Joan's nursing training at St Thomas' Hospital. Duty, service, absolute cleanliness, strict discipline are not what hospitals are famous for today.

This nursing training was a step on the way to Joan's dream of service in India. Here she worked in Calcutta where she met with Mahatma Gandhi, attending his prayer meetings and supporting his fast in the villages. After that came what is now Pakistan and battles over birth control. Finally hands-on work took her to community nursing in one of the poorest parts of America where to be able to ride a horse was as important as being able to push in a hypodermic needle.

This is a panoramic life on a journey of great compassion and academic achievement.

Bruce Kent

Bruce Kent 2002

ACKNOWLEDGEMENTS

Many people have given generously of their time to help me launch this book which I was inspired to complete by John Latham, the poet, who read earlier chapters and told me to go off and finish it. So I did. I am grateful for the encouragement of my friends particularly Nicola Carmichael, Elizabeth Anderson, my American cousin Carol Gibson-Smith, Bridget Leneghan, and many others who kept my spirits up when I felt the task was too daunting.

Others, particularly Ken Hill, Wayne Olsen, Pat Griffin, Diana Wilson and Vanessa Clarke gave invaluable practical help in preparing the manuscript, and thanks are also due to Trudi Tate for helpful advice and criticism.

I am especially grateful to Bruce Kent for agreeing to write the preface to this book, and for his interest and support.

Above all, I owe a great debt to Donna Parsons, my editor who took the original script away, edited it and helped me make sense of my story, which I myself have found confusing at times, and to Greta Ling, assistant editor, for her competence and enthusiasm.

If you live through the imagination, as I do, but also have training and practical ability to push for social change, then you may be destined to be a pioneer and to live dangerously, as I have. To all those who love me, or have loved me over the years, and stood by me, I shall always be grateful, as I am to all the dear companions, especially my cats, who sing me to sleep at night, and help me to believe that life is worth living.

The author and publishers also wish to thank the following for permission to reprint copyright material: A.P. Watt Ltd on behalf of The National Trust for Places of Historical Interest or Natural Beauty for extracts from *Kim* by Rudyard Kipling.

For Nicola Carmichael

CONTENTS

INTRODUCTION

I was born 83 years ago into an "upper class" family in London. My mother, who was an alcoholic, loved my brother and me, but she was physically and emotionally abusive, and my father, from whom she was separated, committed suicide. Childhood experiences led me in later life to train as a nurse midwife and a social worker specialising in child protection.

As a child, my escape from sordid reality was through books and the power of imagination, and I was greatly influenced by Kipling. India became my Mecca. I identified closely with Mahatma Gandhi, the movement for Indian Independence, and with Indian writers and poets, and I wanted to go to Bengal to work with the poor and deprived mothers and children. In 1945 I went to Bengal with a Quaker unit and started a midwifery service in the Calcutta slums. I attended Gandhi's prayer meetings and met him again when he was fasting for peace in the villages.

Over the years I became increasingly radical, and campaigned on a number of political issues. Not least, over the last twenty years in campaigning for animal rights. I regard the torture of animals in laboratories and factory farms for instance as an outrageous abuse of power and morally indefensible. This will be the subject of my next book as this one ends in 1977 when I came to Cambridge to read for a degree and so started a new life at the age of 60. I agree with Albert Camus that "it is the writer's responsibility to speak for those who cannot speak for themselves" and I am proud to be an "enemy of the state" and of a government which sanctions and condones unspeakable suffering on the non-human creatures who are victims of its tyranny.

Joan Court
Cambridge 2002

JOAN COURT

Photograph courtesy of the Daily Telegraph

CHAPTER ONE
KNIGHTSBRIDGE
1919 - 1923

Mother's physical appearance was never quite embodied in my mind, perhaps because there was no pleasant physical contact between us, so that I shrank from her even when she was sober. When she was drunk I associated her touch with being shaken, hit or punched, and I thought she smelt unpleasant, I suppose of drink and the cigarettes she smoked constantly. But she had a moleskin coat which I loved and when she was out I often cuddled it against my face, "probably the only warm thing about her", my analyst said forty years later. Mother, who adored animals, could not be expected in those days to associate a fur coat with the live animals killed to make it.

Mother was quite tall, fair haired with remarkable pale, china blue eyes, a slightly beaked nose and clear white skin. She was very beautiful as a young girl and had a lovely soprano voice. She sang to the troops in St Martin-in-the-Fields in the First World War and sometimes sang to me when she was sober, gently romantic songs of the 1920s, "Roses are for loving in the days of June", "Somewhere a voice is calling", "All the little pansy faces look at you with eyes of love", and "In Zanzibar, great land of glory". I have never been able to trace these songs.

From a very early age I sensed that mother was unhappy and this made my feelings towards her more complicated than those of my brother, who detested her and, I learnt more recently, resented the excuses I made for her drinking as we got older. I remember thinking she had sad feet, the heels of her shoes were always worn down at the side.

The first years of our lives were very sheltered. Peter, my brother, two years my senior, was born in 1917. I followed on the 13th April 1919. We lived with our parents in Knightsbridge Square, a cul-de-sac near Harrod's. We saw the Harrod's van drawn by a sturdy bay horse come to our door and sometimes we were allowed to go out and feed the horse sugar lumps. Father, a successful solicitor in the family firm, with offices above the old Fortnum & Mason building at 101 Piccadilly, still lived with us. Peter told me that when he was older he frequently visited father's office and that it was very dark because Fortnum's enormous royal crest blocked the window. I have only fleeting memories of father at that time as we children spent most of our time in the nursery or being taken for walks by Nanny in Kensington Gardens and Regent's Park whilst our parents lived quite separate lives from us.

The atmosphere in the house may have been tense but we were insulated from it, living as we did on the third floor where we had our own bedroom and nursery. We had our meals up there with Nanny but came down to see our parents after tea, boiled eggs and bread and butter fingers and sponge cakes. In the sitting room I was mystified by the sound coming out of the gramophone's great horn. My only memory of mother then was her restraining me from pulling a kitten out from under the sofa by its tail - my first lesson in treating animals gently and of mother's regard for them.

Peter was five years old and I was three when our parents separated in 1922. Mother told me later that father "had another woman" and this could well have been so, but relatives say that mother was drinking heavily from the time she married and that she was often dangerously violent towards him. By all accounts they were an ill-matched pair, not only sexually, although I think that was an important factor, but temperamentally. Mother was vivacious, caustic, quick-witted and impatient. Father, slow, pedantic, deliberate in thought and action, "he always chewed his food twenty times a bite" mother said and he liked to browse for hours in bookshops and stationery departments. He was also, I am told, an extremely hard worker and probably spent long hours away from home. I understood later that he had a typically depressive temperament, placatory and passive, which mother would have found infuriating. "He was too good to live", said his brother, my Uncle Jack who was a cold fish. Uncle Jack also told me that my mother had ruined my father's life for him. "Do you know your mother used to chase him round the room with a carving knife?" he said, as if it was my fault. Father must have been one of the first battered husbands.

My brother and I remember father leaving . The atmosphere must have been highly charged because of the vivid impression it left with us. We stood at the top of the nursery stairs waving goodbye, mother, servants, and us children. I understood that father was supposed to be returning after the weekend but

I did not believe it. Too young to reason intellectually, I sensed something was very wrong. Peter and I were given gas-filled balloons, I assume to distract us, and we both remember them floating up to the ceiling out of reach.

Mother was given legal custody of Peter and me at the time of the legal separation, probably because she was the legally wronged party and it was customary at that time for mothers to be given custody of the children, especially daughters, when parents separated. Later Peter spent at least half of his school holidays with father and his family and this may have been part of the legal arrangement. No such arrangements were made for me so I did not see father again for seven years. No one, except mother, ever talked about him to me again, and as her remarks were always despairing or derogatory, there were no bridges across the chasm that separated him from me. When I was older he wrote to me sometimes from court, little notes that I treasured but did not fully understand, as I could not picture how or where he worked.

CHAPTER TWO

PARSONAGE FARM

1922 - 1923

Mother then had charge of Peter and me, and at first we went to stay in a hotel. I remember we got out of bed one evening and went down a great staircase in our nightclothes to look for mother and caused some consternation when we appeared in the dining room.

Quite soon we all went to live at Parsonage Farm, our maternal grandparents' home in Rickmansworth until more permanent arrangements could be made. We were there for about a year, and I remember it as a period of undiluted happiness. Grandma told me later that mother was drinking methylated spirits at the time as she was prevented from buying other alcohol, but Peter and I saw little of her. We slept at the far end of the rambling house in the nursery wing, and were cared for by grandma and the servants; our beloved Mrs Smith, the cook, and the parlour maids Eileen and Ellen. If the weather was bad Mrs Smith brought us up a bowl of dough to play with and Peter had a meccano set; we had clay pipes and soapy water for blowing bubbles. When we were unwell Mrs Smith cooked us little delicacies, beef tea, prettily shaped fruit jellies, tiny pink blancmanges and honey in lemon juice.

When we were children, the pink washed farm with its great Elizabethan chimney looked over gardens and pasture, the barns, dairy and medieval granary. The gravel drive was bordered with French poplars and high hedges but we usually took the short cut through the paddock to the station. Beside the drive opposite the paddock grew a magnificent hornbeam tree. The putting lawn at the front was edged with standard rose trees, grandpa's pride and joy, and a splendid Wellington tree dominated the lawn where we had tea in the summer, cucumber sandwiches, bread and jam, scones and Fuller's coffee cake, all carried out on a silver tray by Ellen. At the back of the house was a wild garden and a field for the Clumber dogs and their kennels and we built a play home in a holly tree.

Parsonage Farm is a scheduled building, recorded in the Doomsday Book, but recently "developed" into single flats; the Elizabethan barns destroyed to make room for smart pseudo-Georgian town houses, and the house itself a gutted, reconstituted façade of its former glory. The hornbeam tree was still standing until very recently, patched and propped up, subject to a protection order, a solitary sad relic in what was once the drive, but is now a car park for the occupants of the ersatz little houses which crowd round the farm. No wonder the tree died. It was no longer there when I prowled round this year, angry and lamenting the loss of so much beauty. As far as I am concerned "development" is a rude word, equated with mindless destruction.

But in 1923 when Peter and I spent that happy year there all was undisturbed and we were left to play and occupy ourselves all day as we wished. We spent many greedy afternoons following Parsons the gardener and his cat, gorging ourselves on gooseberries, blackcurrants and peaches. Peter and I liked watching the chickens and searching in the barns and disused pig sties for eggs. There was always a basket of fresh eggs in the kitchen and the gentle cows came home every night, padding their way into their stalls ready to be milked.

Even more than the farm it was the house I loved with its benign influence and sense of peace and it has remained obsessively in my mind, as it has in Peter's, throughout our lives. The stone flagged kitchen was enormous with a long oak table down the centre and an oak dresser for the Italian blue and white kitchen china. I would sit happily there, on the Windsor arm chair, watching Mrs Smith at work or helping Ellen dry up the silver in one of the tiny sculleries, looking out on to the wild garden.

The peaceful sun-filled rooms, with roses and sweet peas reflected in the highly polished mahogany and rosewood tables, the antique dial clock ticking the regular hours, the shining copper and brass and the warm Turkish carpets underfoot all combined to make me feel secure and happy. The curious presence of the resident ghost, a monk, whose flapping sandals could be heard on the lino in the passage upstairs especially when the apples were being stored and he was disturbed, gave a feeling of timelessness in keeping with the history of the house. It was an ordered life. The gong sounded regularly for meals and I had no reason to suppose things would not go on like this for ever. No one explained to us what had happened or what was going to happen.

Our lives were not enriched with human love (except from the servants) as our grandparents tended to treat us as "poor Muriel's children" and some of their disapproval and no doubt worry was displaced on us. I sensed even then that we were regarded as inferior compared to our cousins Monica, Bridget and Patrick, the children of our mother's younger sister, Marjorie. This feeling of being in some way stigmatised was not imagined because it was noticed by the servants. As Ellen, the parlour maid, told me later, "we tried to make it up to you, without making you feel there was anything wrong", and indeed they did, by showing an interest in us and with little attentions to our well-being.

I doubt if Peter was even aware of it but there was also the absurd snobbery voiced by the grandparents and mother towards father and his family, as "the Courts" were not regarded as having come from "the top drawer". I remember being told, as if it was the gravest social failing, that father and his family drank beer on the river when they lived in Maidenhead, and that father wore a made up tie, "so common" mother was always saying, about this and his other social failings. In the face of such class snobbery it is surprising that mother married into the Court family. It was explained to me that mother's family rented a house each summer by the river and "it was a case of propinquity" as father and his family lived next door, and he was invited over (surely most injudiciously) with his brother to play tennis with "the Gibson girls". So Peter and I were not only the children of the family scapegoat, mother, but also had a vulgar father. I am sure our grandparents did their best to be fair, but children are not easily deceived and I was certainly conscious of their covert attitude. Abused children usually suffer from "guilt by association" as if their parents' failings or perceived shortcomings had contaminated them and this is particularly so in cases of sexual abuse. But this vague feeling of being an outcast did not then weigh heavily on me.

Grandma, known for some reason as Baa Baa, sat most of the day on the sofa smoking Craven A cigarettes, using a green enamelled cigarette holder. For at least thirty years of her life she sat on the sofa most of the day. She had been told she must rest because of heart trouble, an order she took literally, never raising her hand to exert herself. There was little necessity, waited on as she was by servants. She would occasionally walk to the bottom of the drive with me and once a week she took us to the cinema, but we were driven there by Giles in the Daimler and she was carefully placed in the car, a rug tucked around her knees. She would then grip the gold tassel hanging by the window and instruct Giles to go slowly, never more than twenty miles an hour.

Grandpa, also known as Cuckoo, a most idiotic name for a magnificently good looking six-footer, vanished soon after breakfast to work and at weekends went shooting or for a round of golf at Moor Park or perhaps to see his mistress as I learnt later. Perhaps Baa Baa had reason to retire into the role of invalid. It must have been a difficult marriage for her, as her earlier life was quite adventurous, brought up in the wilds of Canada where her father, an engineer, was building the Trans-Canadian railway and the family lived under pioneering conditions. "You could hear the wolves prowling around" grandma told us.

Grandpa managed the farm as a side line and indeed he had a great feeling for the land and the countryside although he desecrated it in his work and by engaging in blood sports. But he was also the general manager of the Metropolitan Surplus Lands Company, a company that he formed at the end of World War One. He had a grand office in the station premises where he travelled daily from Rickmansworth. We children sometimes travelled with him and he used his "gold" concession card so we sailed haughtily by the ticket barrier to his office where his attending secretary greeted him and us with maternal respect. Grandpa kept his faithful servants and secretaries for a lifetime, but he made no provision for them at all in his will, not even for Mrs Smith who worked for him for thirty years.

On the huge table in his office there were models of the housing "developments" the Company was planning, intriguing to us children at the time, less so now. I wonder if my hatred of suburbia has something to do with resentment that grandpa helped to disfigure the countryside by promoting ugly rows of villas in Pinner, Northwood Hills and Moor Park whilst himself living in the most beautiful house I have ever seen.

But I was inordinately boastful about grandfather when I was young. I thought he owned all the trains and railways in the country and I felt a great surge of veneration whenever I saw a steam train chugging by, or heard one hooting in the night from my room at the farm. And ever since then, when I have not been abroad, I have managed to rent and later buy homes near to the railway, gentrified Victorian cottages (not of course suburban), the last and best being my home in Cambridge where I can even hear the voice on the loudspeaker announcing the arrival and departure of trains.

Grandpa gave me a sense of material security, no small thing, and he radiated all the confidence of the Edwardian male and the established order and this combined with his wealth, success and not least of all his beautiful possessions impressed me deeply. Grandpa had a marvellous eye for antiques which he collected over the years. Some of these antiques he inherited from his mother.

Great granny, Annie Gibson, was a formidable character; heiress to a considerable fortune inherited from her father, the banker Ashwell. She and great grandpa lived with their four sons and Annie their daughter, who later married Gordon Craig the revolutionary theatre designer (son of Ellen Terry the actress who lived in Hatfield and was great grandma's best friend at that time). The great grandparents lived in Ashwell House, an enormous Victorian mansion in St Albans, now a Masonic headquarters. When her children married, great grandma, who had a penchant for buying property, gave each of them £6000 and a house. She gave grandpa and Penelope, his new bride, Bleak House in St Albans, an elegant Georgian house, now the headquarters of the County Social Services. Grandpa became Mayor of St Albans and an auctioneer of antiques, so adding to his collection. Now, at Parsonage Farm, these treasures were beautifully kept and polished by Eileen and Ellen and the Parliament clock in the smoking room ticked peacefully, watching over us with its great, open, parchment coloured face.

It was some years before I came to distance myself from grandpa's values, whilst retaining my intense love for Parsonage Farm, my earthly paradise. I grew to reject and spurn his racial prejudices. "Don't you dare ever bring a black man or a Jew into this house", he once told me, perhaps beginning to suspect I might have deviant views. He also warned me about the dangers of being too familiar with the servants, remarking that "they don't respect you for it, you know, and they'll take advantage".

But the first major erosion of my identification with him and all he stood for came later, over the question of blood sports, not before I was nine or ten, and it did not stop me continuing to visit Parsonage Farm. The great shoots in Scotland where our grandfather went each year as a member of a syndicate with Bernard Ducker and other tycoons, were occasions of much activity and excitement at the Farm, with Mrs Smith packing food hampers and grandpa cleaning and polishing his guns.

On one occasion I went with him on a local shoot near Chorleywood. I had seen him bring back dead and bloody pheasants and grouse, they usually hung for a while in the smoking room before being transferred to the kitchen, but I had never seen one die before I went out with him. I saw him aim his gun, heard the shot, then a free flying pheasant suddenly plummeted from the sky. I was appalled and shocked, and knew I was part of a wicked act as I looked at the murdered bird, limp and bloodstained, placed carefully at our feet by the retriever dog. I must have appeared upset as grandpa laughed and patted my head, but I said nothing. I suppose unconsciously I did not want to fall out with him and as I had no model of benign authority I was afraid of challenging him or telling him what I thought about it. Children of nine or ten with stable backgrounds are more confident but I lacked this sort of confidence and indeed had every reason to fear authority. The fear has remained with me as a residual handicap so that I have frequently tried to be seen as "respectable" and "sound" by those in authority whilst at the same time supporting causes and pioneering ventures which were or are ahead of their time and inimical to the establishment such as pacifism, family planning and animal rights . As I describe my later career the corrosive effect of early childhood suffering on my ability to do what I wanted and felt to be right will become apparent as will the various conscious and unconscious ways I found to be both an iconoclast and a conformer.

Parsonage Farm

Parsonage Farm in later years

Grandfather
Henry Gibson

CHAPTER THREE

BAKER STREET

1924 - 1926

Life at Parsonage Farm was but a brief respite between the break-up of our parents' marriage and the establishment of a home with mother in a flat at the back of Baker Street station provided by our grandfather although there is no reason to suppose that father did not pay the bills.

The only reason I have for supposing that this and our subsequent moves were traumatic is that I can recall nothing about them at all, the actual transition from one place to another is wiped clean from my mind. I have though, all my life, felt an exaggerated dread whenever I have to leave or return home, as if some terrible disaster hangs over me. This has not prevented me, and indeed may have caused me to travel extensively, perhaps in an effort to conquer the fear by reliving it or just, as Freudians would undoubtedly say, through some form of repetition compulsion. Not by chance, I am sure, I live in Cambridge, a city which each year goes through the rituals of departure and return as the students "come up" or "go down".

As my Siamese cat Pushkin would comment if she could "Why can't loved ones all stay in one place for ever". A sensible view of things I have not emulated.

I was four years old when we moved to the Baker Street flat. It was on the fourth floor of Clarence Gate Gardens, Malcombe Street and we could see Madame Tussaud's from the window, or perhaps I have imagined this, as what I actually remember is the excitement the night it caught fire. There was a bathroom on the right of the entrance hall, then the kitchen and sitting room at the end of a passage, with two bedrooms on the left. We never used the bathroom, sitting room or the spare bedroom. Peter and I shared a bedroom with mother, who may have been afraid of sleeping alone and we ate and sat in the kitchen. I remember the flat as cold as if it was always winter.

Quite soon it must have been decided that Peter was "uncontrollable". Mother said he kept giving her "black looks" and he sometimes kicked and punched her when she attacked him. He was sent to a preparatory school at Clifton. I do not remember his actual departure as I have totally repressed the memory of this and similar painful separations but when he came back for part of his holidays I felt much safer although I often feared for his safety. Mother would send him out to buy her cigarettes and I would sit at the window as darkness fell, afraid he would never come back. I have remained uneasy when I am indoors as evenings draw in until the lights are on and the curtains drawn and I worry excessively when loved ones are late coming home, including of course the cats.

These were terrible years. We were too young to understand what enraged mother. We knew she would be all right in the morning, but by afternoon she was strange. It was as if we had two mothers. She would mutter to herself and make faces, start crying and fall over the furniture. Then something would spark her off, perhaps the very presence of us children, and she would explode into a terrible rage, grabbing us and shrieking at us as we tried to escape. I do not remember the actual moment of any of her attacks, or the pain, but I once had evidence of how the terror was encapsulated in my mind when I relived it in a brief psychotic experience forty years later. But consciously I only remember trying to dodge her flailing arms and the hairbrush she used to hit us with. Trying to escape only enraged her further and sometimes Peter just stood in stony and grim silence glaring at her. He said I made it worse by trying to get away and crying.

Peter learnt when he was very little ways of dealing with bullies. I am not surprised he survived so well in adult life when he was a prisoner of war in a Japanese camp in Korea. "Anyone who has been in an English public school learns how to survive", he said, but I think he learnt his stoicism in another school.

I was impressed, perhaps over-impressed, by Peter's superior knowledge and confidence. For example, he told me that the reason my head hurt was because I had a headache and I was reassured that the ache had a name and a cause. Then when he came back from his first term at school he would sometimes talk about his new experiences and I would respond to his evident enthusiasm, pretending to understand what he was saying. His authority and evident wisdom and the fact that I felt so much safer when he was there has affected, not surprisingly, all my subsequent relationships with men whom I continue to regard as ultimately more powerful, competent and knowledgeable than I, in spite of evidence to the contrary.

When Peter was away mother was less violent, though she was still strange and given to sudden maelstroms of rage, so that I rarely felt safe. I do not remember ever going out without her, but she was away from the flat for long periods herself. No one visited us then, not even Grandma, although in later years she called round to see us every two weeks. It has only recently occurred to me to wonder why Grandpa never came, considering that his office was only a hundred yards or so away. Both of them were well aware that mother was an alcoholic. They must have decided to wash their hands of any further responsibility for us once we left their care, at least during those vulnerable years when we were least able to take care of ourselves. I do not know why father made no contact at this time although Peter must have been visiting him.

When mother was out of the house I was able to retreat into my imaginary world, a world contained in my toy farmyard. Perhaps it brought back memories of Parsonage Farm. I became absorbed, sitting at the kitchen table with the precious lead animals: the black and white cows, some standing, some lying down, the great brown cart horses, the noble brilliantly coloured turkey, the sheep and the little chickens, the farm buildings, white and green gates and fences and the two dimensional trees. One of the resting cows had a dent in her side and I worried about her and I always put her safely near a fence so she would not get hurt again. The farm animals were die cast lead, painted, made by a firm called Model Home Farm, as I discovered last year when I visited the Bethnal Green Museum of Childhood. I was transfixed when I saw them there, longing to claim them as my own.

I also had Simpson, a little dark striped tabby cat who kept me constant company. I owe so much of my mental and emotional health to Simpson and his beloved successors. Cats have always been my bulwark and a symbol of all that is warm, loving, dignified, free and beautiful and I never feel quite safe or happy without one (or more) at hand. I have five now, and sleep with the Siamese, "Pushkin", in the crook of my arm and Mimi and Lucy at my feet. Simpson, purring loudly, would walk across the table knocking over a few cows and chickens en route, but I loved him too much to care and would patiently re-assemble my farm when he had settled on my lap.

Mother frequently did not return until after dark. I could not reach to light the gas mantle and in any case preferred to be in bed when she returned. So Simpson and I would get into bed and I pushed him down to the bottom under the bedclothes and hoped he would not be discovered. I avoided touching him with my feet so he would be less likely to purr. Not that mother would have harmed him, but she did not allow him to sleep in my bed.

I have only one memory of anyone calling. I never saw a postman or a milkman. On that one occasion I was in bed when there was a soft knock on the front door and a neighbour crept in to ask if I was all right. I could see she was frightened and she asked me not to tell mother that she had called. I understood her fear and in the years to come other neighbours occasionally made tentative efforts to intervene or console us but no one ever dared to take any action to protect us.

I was usually awake when mother came in although I pretended to be asleep. Sometimes she would leave me alone and I would take great care not to move or make a sound. But if she was still in a maudlin stage she probably felt lonely and wanted some response from me. She would tell me to get up and her mood would change with alarming and terrifying suddenness and she would scream and rant and beat me with the clothes brush, pull my hair and pinch my arms. I now know that she was subject to violent rages even as a child so I imagine that alcohol only released the aggression and frustration she had always felt, particularly against her parents and husband. Later when I was about ten years old she told me that grandpa had tried to make love to her when she was a child, but I would not listen to her thinking that this was just another of her perverse sexual fantasies. Now I see no reason to doubt her, particularly as grandpa once made an erotic approach to me, when I was twelve or thirteen, admiring and touching my breasts, when I was in bed, wearing one of grandma's satin nighties and drinking early morning tea. I must have frozen him off as the episode was not repeated. I did not though, put two and two together, in regard to mother, as I would now, understanding as I do the seeds of destruction that may have led to her addiction and cruelty.

When Peter was away at boarding school I could not get mother into bed and she would have to stay where she collapsed, usually on the bedroom or kitchen floor. If Peter was there we usually managed to heave her on to the bed. On my own I was sometimes frightened thinking she had died and I would try to revive her with smelling salts, half glad that she was no longer screaming and shouting and lashing out at me, but I was also afraid of the uncanny silence when she sank into an alcoholic coma.

So the months went by and except when Peter came home I lived in a world shadowed by fear relieved only when I was alone in the house with Simpson and my farmyard. All my life I have loved living alone with my pets and attempts to share my home permanently from time to time have not been very successful. It is always a great joy to come home after a tough working day to a house occupied only by my non-human friends.

We left Baker Street about two years later, I think grandpa wanted the tenancy of the flat back, and whilst he was arranging for a permanent home for us we stayed for a brief time in a furnished room in a boarding house in High Wycombe, where I suppose Simpson could not be with us. I was told that he had been given to a nice farm home. I did not believe this and I was haunted for the next fifty years by a vision of him being dumped in a country road and walking all alone trying to find a place to stay. For some crazy reason this was exemplified for me whenever I saw the advertisement for "Start Rite Shoes" showing two little children, a boy and a girl, walking off into the far distance. They always look sad to me, not equipped, even with their sensible shoes, to manage on their own.

Nowadays, working with abused children and their families I always try to make sure the children are not worried about pets they may leave behind when they come into care. It may not always be possible to re-unite them but at least the children are not left in the dark about them. Social workers tend to regard a child's love of a companion animal as a substitute for satisfactory human relationships and although this is partially true, as it is to a significant degree for me, or was when I was a child, I am convinced that relationships between people and animals are far more complex than is generally realised. The death or loss of a pet even in "normal" families can be a major trauma both to adults and children. Animals are usually perceived as true members of the family but the rich complexity of these relationships is poorly understood by the so-called helping professions and it is only recently that it has become of interest to academics. It is as if it is somehow sentimental or wrong to give time and attention to animals when there is so much human suffering in the world, a blinkered, ignorant and irrational view I find quite infuriating.

CHAPTER FOUR

PINNER

1926

I started school when we were at High Wycombe. Mother, who seemed happier, took me round to see various establishments and we visited a very quiet and lovely school outside the town with empty shadowed classrooms with neat rows of desks (it must have been the school holidays) a library and a chapel. I felt a sense of longing to be part of the place, the first hint of a life-long hunger for education but mother said "we can't afford it, darling" and I was enrolled in quite a rough town school, or so it seemed to me. But then I had had no contact with other children except for Peter, and I did not know what was expected of me and had no idea how to make friendly contact. I visit infant schools quite often nowadays and I find it therapeutic just to sit and absorb the amazing life and vitality around me, the colour and music, the sight of small children sitting in small groups absorbed in their projects. It was not like that seventy years ago. On my first morning I sat in front of a large poster with some incomprehensible pictures and symbols on it, silently weeping with bewilderment. In the weeks to follow I settled down and I am grateful to the teacher who kept me in after school and made me learn to read, patiently and firmly breaking through my fear and resistance.

Meanwhile mother had found an admirer, and although I cannot remember him clearly, I thought he was nice, and enjoyed it when he took us out for picnics in the woods, my first sight of bluebells, and later, in the autumn, we went blackberrying, accompanied by his cheerful mongrel dog. Mother, in this brief period, must have either stopped drinking or greatly restricted the amount she drank, a curious interlude in our lives.

In 1926, we moved to Pinner, to 7 Stanley Villas, Marsh Lane, a few minutes from the station with the railway running close to the back of the house. There was a small triangular garden, with an apple tree, and peonies in the flower beds. When Peter was home we spent many hours reading in the garden, he engrossed in "The Magnet" or "The Boys' Own Paper" and I in "The

Rainbow" and stories of Buffalo Bill. We were enthralled with stories about India and father sent us both all the Kipling stories. I think we wove our separate fantasies about India as I do not remember talking about it together, but from very early days we were both intent to go there once we were grown up, as indeed we did. We were both compulsive readers and my idea of purgatory is to be landed somewhere without anything to read, a situation which has actually happened only twice in my life, once when I was stranded overnight in a bus station in America, and once in Turkey in a remote leprosy clinic near Mount Ararat when the essential paperbacks were left by mistake in the main baggage stored in the jeep parked miles away. I would rather read a railway timetable than nothing at all.

I know mother resented living in such a squalid little place but when she complained to grandpa about it he said, "You're lucky to have a roof over your head". Lonely and resentful she soon began drinking heavily again.

Our grandparents told us that we could come to Parsonage Farm whenever we liked. I think that by now grandma was worried about us being alone with mother when she was drunk, as she had started visiting in Pinner fortnightly, driving up in the Daimler, staying a short while and giving me half a crown, so she must have felt some concern. We would await our opportunity to slip out of the house to the station, seldom before evening. Mother sometimes followed us and we hid in the alleyways and sometimes in the station master's office until the train to Rickmansworth drew in. It was a steam train in those days, with single carriages and the journey took about an hour, door-to-door. In the school terms I went alone, escaping from mother with an excuse to go and buy her cigarettes. I must have been terrified she would catch me, as the psychotic experience I mentioned earlier, the only one I have ever experienced, occurred when I was travelling by myself in a single railway carriage to work forty years later. Suddenly I felt a sense of mounting terror and mother's furious and annihilating presence as if she was actually in the compartment. I felt compelled to escape by throwing myself out of the door. But I was saved by the life-giving force that has always sustained me, or by my guardian angel, so instead of throwing myself out of the train I sat on the floor head well down and prayed the evil projection would go. Fortunately it was not long before we reached Walthamstow and somewhat shaken I went to the clinic and prepared for my first client. This episode did not come quite out of the blue as I was depressed at the time but it is an example of how memories of childhood traumas may erupt quite dangerously in later life.

Once at Rickmansworth, we would run down the sloping road, under the railway bridge and then cross the road to the paddock leading on to the farm, already visible through the trees promising warmth, comfort and safety, perhaps in the same way as a distressed child perceives the security of its mother's arms. A brief respite until mother came to fetch us home.

In winter at the farm there would be a great log fire burning in the smoking room and in the bathroom warm towels on a heated rail. But before dinner Ellen would bring a polished copper jug of hot water, covered with a towel, to my bedroom. In Pinner the bath, though not literally filled with coal was cracked and yellow and unused other than as a table top or a seat. The kitchen sink where we washed was usually filled with dirty dishes and milk bottles. The place stank because although mother was obsessionally tidy, the sparse ornaments carefully placed, she had not been brought up to do housework or to cook and she never learnt. But then she probably did not notice the filth and squalor. The basic food she provided may partly account for my good health as we never had puddings or cakes except at the farm. Peter remembers both the flat and the house at Pinner smelling of cabbage, but I think it was just the combination of dirt and mildewed washing, left in the copper to moulder from one week to the next.

There were rats in the garden and the kitchen swarmed with flies in the summer. Some struggled and died on the sticky fly papers which were constantly getting entangled in my hair. I thought the flies died a cruel death and sometimes tried to rescue them, but then they came apart and this made me sadder and did not help them. But the one thing we did not have to cope with as children was being needlessly exposed to cruelty to animals. Mother was infinitely compassionate to all creatures, apart from flies, and disapproved of blood sports. She taught me to respect all life, "only God can create life" she would say and tenderly rescue dying beetles who had fallen on their backs and could not get to their feet and she left the spiders undisturbed. I thought of her this spring when I found a furry caterpillar floating on the garden pond. It must have fallen in whilst looking for a drink. It lay inert in the palm of my hand but as the sun warmed it and I blew on its fur ruffling it gently, it gradually began to curl and uncurl and its life returned. Mother would have approved. One of my last memories of her is of trying to dab insect repellent on a horse being plagued by flies. Her concern extended to flowers and she would walk miles with bunches of drooping bluebells, that had been dropped by careless trippers, looking for a stream to place them in and she would top up flower vases in tea shops, as indeed I do.

We did not have a cat in Pinner, just a decrepit mongrel dog called Mutt, who slept in mother's room (where I also had a bed) in a wicker chair that creaked and crackled in the night as Mutt moved about. I did not like dogs much at the time, perhaps I was repelled by Mutt's smell and eczema and his constant scratching.

We were often cold. I had constant sore throats and colds and my legs and hands were often blue and mottled. Mother's allowance from father came at the beginning of the week and we were usually out of food and coal by the weekend, mother having spent the money on drink. She would send me with a note to borrow money from the vicar or a neighbour and I think I was more resentful than embarrassed - resentful of the vicar in his cosy house and what I felt to be his patronising manner, "There, that's something for your dinner then", he would say, reading mother's note with a perplexed look on his face. Peter or I were then sent to buy coal at half a crown a bag from the shop in Station Road.

I was now enrolled in a small local school, an adapted private house with about thirty pupils, a headmistress and two or three teachers. I dreaded the end of the school day, not only because the house was cold and unwelcoming but because I knew mother would have been drinking. At first she would put on a show of sobriety but my heart sank when I heard the slight slur in her speech that heralded a change in consciousness and in her behaviour. The transformation was usually quite sudden and quite terrifying. I feared her violence but I was also increasingly disgusted by the maudlin stage as I grew older as I thought it was undignified and embarrassing. She would weep and cling to me and I would try to comfort her but I felt repelled. I would make tea but it was a charade because she slopped the tea and banged the cup in the saucer and she was not really there. I knew I could not reach her and make her better. I would stir in the sugar, fetch her cigarettes and pretend there was nothing wrong, but she would sink into gloom and then suddenly erupt into violence, ranting and raving and threatening to flay me alive. She threw crockery and bottles about until the kitchen or bedroom was strewn with breakages. Her expression was hideous with hate and her long fingers like talons grabbed my hair and scratched my arms and face. When she lapsed into unconsciousness she would snore on the bed but in the early hours I would hear her vomiting and she would moan for me to help her and then to wind up her dank hair in curling rags. At first I pretended not to hear her but in the end I always got up because I wanted to stop her moaning voice calling,

"Joan, Joan.." with a plaintive wail. By then the chamber pot by the bed would be full of foaming red vomit - mother usually drank Burgundy - perhaps this was the cheapest alcohol available.

I remember one particular evening when Peter was at boarding school, by then at Berkhamstead Public School, mother and I were in the front bedroom and it was dark apart from the light in the street. She was lying comatose on the bed reeking of drink and urine. The room was a shambles, the floor littered with glass and broken ornaments and the gas mantle was broken. I looked at myself in the mirror by the light of the street lamp. My arms were covered in bruises and a rash from being beaten with the clothes brush. I wore a short pink cotton dress and my hair, neatly cropped, fell over a calm, round, pale face. I said to myself, suddenly conscious, perhaps for the first time, of my identity, that when I was grown up I would "do something about children", but I also felt a premonition that my own childhood would exact a price and cast shadows in the future.

By then I had discovered the meditations of Marcus Aurelius, which became like a Bible to me, and I recited to myself, "When force of circumstance upsets your equanimity, lose no time in recovering your self-control and do not remain out of tune longer than you can help". With this dictum in mind I would then sweep up and tidy and as I cleared up the breakages, I would think, "Be like the headland against which the waves break and break; it stands firm until presently the watery tumult around it subsides and once more to rest." I would rejoice that mother would be out for the count until dawn and I could go down to the kitchen and read.

But I did not consistently apply the precepts of the noble Roman lord to all my behaviour and it sometimes occurred to me that Marcus Aurelius would not approve of stealing. By then I was quite an experienced thief. But my second mentor, Dick Turpin, would approve. I was an avid reader of Dick Turpin paperbacks which cost two shillings and sixpence each from the station bookshop. But I took from the Stoics much of what I needed for survival and mental health and the motto "Thou shall endure". This led to an attitude of arrogance and disdain which was not in the character of Marcus Aurelius. From very early on I saw myself as capable of great endurance in spite of the terrors and miseries of home life and as set apart from other people by the nature of my upbringing, as indeed I was. As Marcus Aurelius would put it, "Let no emotion of the flesh, be it pain or pleasure, affect the supreme sovereign portion of the soul". Hardly a dictum to encourage conviviality and quite at odds with what I perceive now as my innate nature, hungry and greedy for life and colour.

I cannot remember when I began to steal, though I always took money from mother's purse when I needed it, either when I wanted to buy a book or to get away to Rickmansworth. It is also likely that our strange and irregular meals left me hungry because the first thing I remember stealing was food from Cullen's grocery shop in the High Street. I am sure mother never deliberately kept us short of food but when she was drinking she was not interested in meals and when she was sober she was handicapped by lack of money or housekeeping skills.

I stole cheese and figs from Cullen's and although hunger was probably the original driving force, soon stealing brought its own reward of excitement and comfort. It seemed, if I can recall a mood, to bring a momentary lift of spirits, but I was conscious of guilt and knew quite well that I was doing wrong. Sometimes the thefts were very trivial and could have brought no reward other than the fun of "getting away with it". Abused children tell me now that stealing makes them feel they are alive. For example, I stole buttons from the drapery store and threw them into the River Pinn. I also threw my dinner money into the river but this was because I was too afraid to tell mother I had not used it but had, instead, used the lunch break to race off to the fields to play. I went on stealing intermittently right through my teens until, by then, I was stealing books from shops and libraries and even suitcases from bigger stores. Nowadays I note that they are usually chained up! Unlike most children who steal for neurotic reasons I was never caught and in time, learning something of ethics and morality or perhaps from fear I gave up of my own accord. But I still have a sneaking sympathy for shoplifters and sometimes if I see old ladies in the supermarkets slipping the odd packet of butter or tin of cat food into their bags I distract the girl at the till so that the culprit can escape undetected.

By the age of seven or eight reading was my greatest joy and solace. I collected "Everyman" editions and took to heart their dedication on the fly leaf - "Everyman, I will go with thee, and be thy guide, In thy most need to go by thy side." By then I had discovered not only the Jungle Book, Marcus Aurelius and Dick Turpin but other stories of adventure and rapacity. Soon in my imagination I was galloping on my black horse, masked, and with a cloak streaming in the wind across the moors and fens, lost to the world, or I was with Mowgli climbing the Himalayas and sailing down the Ganges and walking in the jungle with Mother Wolf, with whom I was closely identified. It must have been at about this time that Rin Tin Tin was showing at the cinema. I loved him dearly. He rescued children from the burning forest. He was the wrong sex but the nearest thing to Mother Wolf that I could identify with at that time. In my imagination I half believed that Mother Wolf was my real mother and I, of course, was Mowgli. Recently I met three Siberian wolfhounds walking with their master across Parker's Piece in Cambridge and felt the familiar sense of love and identification, and longed to hug them.

CHAPTER FIVE

GROWING UP

1927

By the age of eight or nine I had discovered not only the joys of reading but of nature, fields of buttercups with gentle horses browsing, butterflies, bird-songs, rabbits, sunlight in the orchards. But books were life-saving and an imaginative escape at home when I was not at Parsonage Farm. These islands of relief were particularly important to me when Peter was away at school. Animals too were, as ever, the greatest comfort. I remember once finding a mother cat, a tabby, deep in a grassy ditch near a farm shaded from prying eyes and the sun. Her arms were round a clutch of little kittens all sucking away and tumbling around her. Her sleepy green eyes barely registered my awed presence as she sang to her babies blinking in the sunlight. I understood instantly the nature of mother love and how it offered protection, comfort and relief from hunger, and for ever after that, the imprint of that revelation of love stayed with me. I became increasingly aware of the infinite beauty and dignity of animals and of my own feelings, a raging protectiveness and tenderness towards them. I always remembered Simpson, without whose benign companionship I would have had no life at all at the Baker Street flat.

There were other respites from mother. I attended school regularly though I continued to learn very little. I made friends who would go out with me, but was not invited to any of their homes and of course neither Peter or I ever had friends round to our house. I remember that on one occasion a girl called Susan took me back home to play and as I stood at the front door I heard her mother say, "I don't want that child in my house". I do not remember feeling hurt but the incident must have made some impression or I would not remember it so clearly. I doubt though if I felt the impact of social ostracism in the same way as I felt denigrated by our grandparents, towards whom I had begun to feel a vague sense of resentment. I thought it unfair of them to favour our cousins, whom grandpa once said, "always work hard and play hard and enjoy themselves". Cousin Monica was especially favoured and grandma sometimes took her with her on expensive holidays by the sea and on shopping expeditions. I must have repressed a lot of jealousy, feeling like an orphanage child, leaning over the gate watching the vicarage children at play unable to join in. My feelings were not clearly differentiated and never expressed but a degree of envy and an over-anxious determination to excel in everything I do, and my delight in achievement show, I think, at least to some degree, a neurotic attempt to repair cracks in my self esteem.

At about this age I began to have romantic fantasies and vague sexual feelings. Mother's views on sex were perverse and revolting and her comments about sex were disturbing. Although she never explained to me what sex was all about, and in those days we were not taught in school, she made it clear that she thought it was disgusting. This conflicted with my own bodily perceptions which were quite exciting and pleasant. I was far too inhibited to ask any questions, so I sought for enlightenment in books, searching through the library for erotic or informative material, without success. Then I discovered some volumes by Marie Stopes in mother's wardrobe, and all was revealed. "Married Love" was the title of one I think. I did not understand all the diagrams, but I grasped the main gist in the text. I at once accepted that the written word was the truth, far more trustworthy than anything mother told me.

But I was affected by her tirades and sometimes found them very frightening. She often spoke of sexual perversions and once told me that a woman had had intercourse with her dog and gave birth to a baby that barked. For some reason this really frightened me, so that years later, the story long forgotten consciously, the memory erupted in analysis with all the encapsulated feelings I must have felt when I was nine. I am appalled to think of what children must suffer in the way of mental trauma and conflict nowadays when they are compelled to watch hard porn video films with their abusers.

Mother told me that she hated father making love to her, "it was like an express train coming at you", she said, "getting faster and faster and then he'd collapse all over me". Marie Stopes could not have made it clear to me what an orgasm was and as I never masturbated, it remained a mystery until I was well into my twenties. Mother talked a great deal about lesbianism and I only half understood what she was talking about, even when she said about my relationship with my best friend, "you're like a dog after a bitch". She told me that I was over-sexed and had unnatural feelings about my friends. By then she was beginning to express an intense jealousy of any relationship I formed and this made me secretive. In adult life I am still very inept at coping with jealousy and possessiveness, even though I have sometimes allowed a relationship to develop which encouraged such feelings.

But on the other hand mother's perception that I had erotic feelings towards my best friend, Rita, was correct. Rita and I would sit in the woods and I would half undress her, cuddle and kiss her and we would sing, "Pale hands I loved beside the Shalimar", and a popular song of that period, "Isn't it romantic?" Interestingly this first love adventure was unmarred by guilt and quite unaffected by the shadow of mother's morbid preoccupations. Rita said, "that's because you are strong minded, I would be upset". I told Rita all about life at home in the way that abused children often do first confide in their friend.

At home too I was also learning ways of coping. I could always go to Rickmansworth, but even when I stayed at home I learnt to turn a deaf ear. It was the era of crystal radios and headphones, rather similar to the personal stereos that young people wear nowadays. I curled up in a chair with headphones clamped to my head and learnt to block out the world's sounds, smiling at my mother when I could not hear a word she said. I retreated into a private world. Later when mother asked me about the programme I had apparently been listening to, I had to make up some story because in fact I had been paying scant attention and often not understood what was being said.

This tuning out had its educational and social drawbacks, combined with the terror of not understanding, or not wanting to understand, what was being said. The terror and tedium of exposure to mother's ranting and raving and the sheer boredom and resentment of the evil tide of filth and hatred she poured out on me when she was drunk, meant that at school I found it impossible to take anything in, though I was often enchanted by the sound of the teacher's calm voice. I sat at the back of the class and devoured comics and particularly one which featured Minnehaha. We were reading Hiawatha at school and I identified with this black haired beauty paddling her canoe down the river. I imagined she lived in India and longed to join her. My fantasies about running away to India began with Mowgli and then became confused with American Indians.

I knew that mother's treatment of me was not personal but came from some inner misery. I sensed in her a sad dependent love towards me, which I felt as a burden, but which made it impossible for me to reject her entirely, as Peter apparently did. Then too I had books which revealed other worlds of personal relationships and gave me an imaginary life and values and there were chance encounters at crucial times, lifebuoys in a troubled sea - so that I did not altogether lack trust in people.

I remember particularly Dr. Sharp in Pinner, our general practitioner. On one occasion he came round when I had a sprained ankle. I was in bed and in some pain and I remember his expression as he looked round the room, which was as usual bare and filthy. Mother was sober but seemed to be responding to my discomfort with a rather callous indifference, I think because I was the centre of attention. She could never bear to see anyone attending to me, a situation that, perhaps fortunately, seldom happened. She made some comment about bathing my foot in cold water and compresses, but Dr. Sharp asked me if hot or cold water would be the most comfortable and I said hot. Whether this materialised or not I cannot remember, but I do remember him instructing mother, and how comforting I found his concern, the gentleness with which he examined me and the fact that he had asked me what I thought would be best.

On another occasion late at night mother had cut herself quite badly on a broken bottle, and bled alarmingly from a wound high up on her thigh. Peter was there at the time and went to fetch Dr. Sharp, who drove back to the house and set about sewing mother's gaping wound while she sat on the wooden bath top. He worked by gaslight quickly and silently, but again I was conscious of his look of compassion and concern as he glanced round the kitchen at the filth and disorder. I knew, although he said nothing, that he understood how things were and I did not resent the fact that he could do nothing about it. It never really occurred to me that anyone could.

We had neighbours but nobody ever intervened, although they must have known what was going on. I do remember once a neighbour in Pinner saying to me, "I could report all this to the NSPCC" and explaining what this meant, but nothing happened, nor did I expect it to though I thought the NSPCC sounded a good idea. Recently a child told me, "They kept telling mother that they'd report her to the NSPCC, but they never did. How I wish they had, then we wouldn't have to stay in this grotty place".

It is strange to think that our relatives let mother take charge of us at all when we were so little and that no-one intervened to protect us. I have rather less resentment now about the fact that Peter and I were allowed to live under such conditions than because nothing was done to help mother, although I could understand people being afraid of her and reluctant to interfere. But why did grandpa not arrange for her to have treatment in a private nursing home? I can only put this down to his meanness over money. He appeared magnanimous but this was part of his charm and had no basis in reality.

We had one neighbour I hated, a singularly unpleasant character who lived next door. I think his name was Dr. Russell. He used to leer at me across the peonies and occasionally tried to kiss me through his revolting eggy moustache. When Peter was "naughty" mother would claim she could not handle him and call Dr. Russell in to beat him. Although Peter's memory is of being sent to Dr. Russell, I remember him coming round to our place, usually in the evening. I sat on the landing outside Peter's bedroom in a state of helpless impotent rage and despair such as I have never felt before or since, listening to the sound of the belt and Peter's screams. I cannot imagine what he was supposed to have done wrong, but he was always less of a passive victim than I was, and less likely to try and placate mother, so he may have defied her, but she also told Dr Russell that, "he's had wet dreams again" and that he must be punished for this.

When Peter was home I did not worry about mother, I simply handed all the responsibility and anxiety over to him. We would try to make mother drunk once she had started on a session because we knew that the sooner she was unconscious the more peaceful it would be. We would then have an interlude before she came to, moaning and vomiting and calling out in her slurred voice. Once we had got her to bed we would hurry down and put on the kettle, search around for burning cigarettes and tip half empty bottles of wine down the sink. On more than one occasion we found an armchair smouldering from a cigarette stub and we would douse it with water making a horrible smell. We picked up the broken china from the dishes mother had thrown at us and turned off the gramophone where Mother had been playing "Kitten on the Keys", "The Minstrel Boy" and "In a Monastery Garden" on the gramophone (although she sometimes sang at the piano). We preferred to be quiet, or to listen to Henry Hall on the radio. We replaced the broken gas mantles, poked the kitchen range and retired into our books. We never had much to say to each other and I now know that Peter thought I made too many excuses for mother as he hated the whole scene and thought it was stupid of me to "stick up" for her.

Quite often we would help ourselves to money from mother's purse and go to Rickmansworth. Sometimes we would arrive very late at night in winter, frozen stiff, and I am told that the maids looking out from their attic bedroom window would say, "Can it be those children coming across the paddock so late?" All in all Peter and I spent a significant part of our lives there, going down frequently as soon as we were old enough to travel by train so that we had a refuge as we grew older, and no longer suffered helplessly as we did when we were too young to escape.

Parsonage Farm meant more to Peter and me than any personal relationship, I think. Once when I said to grandpa that I might like to see my father, he said that if ever I had anything to do with "the Courts" I would no longer be welcome at Parsonage Farm. Not welcome at the farm? There was no question in my mind that I would ever give it up - the gentle stepping cows, the dairy, Parsons the gardener and his cat, the great chestnut trees, Ellen bringing tea on a tray in the morning with wafer thin bread and butter. The farm was our sanctuary and I felt completely at peace there, watching the animals, listening to the dogs barking in the night and stroking the cats as they lay peacefully on the hot pipes in the conservatory.

If Peter or I or both of us arrived at a reasonable hour we would usually be despatched to the kitchen, perhaps because our grandparents had guests and did not want "poor Muriel's dishevelled children" around. Mrs. Smith would prepare ham and eggs and a glass of creamy milk and settle us in chairs with Peg's paper and the wireless. Sometimes we dined with the grandparents. Mrs. Smith was an inspired cook and half a century later my brother and I and our cousins can still recall the wonderful meals she cooked - apple suet puddings, egg custard with grated nutmeg and cream served in little cut glass bowls. At breakfast, punctually served at 9.00am, there was a silver stand of boiled eggs, kept warm with little felt cosies, bacon and eggs, kippers and devilled kidneys, toast and marmalade.

Peter and I remember as if it was yesterday everything to do with Parsonage Farm and especially the amazing Christmases we spent there with our cousins. Coming from our sordid home in Pinner it was a startling contrast, the gleaming table set with scarlet crackers and silver candles and very ornate and wonderful centre pieces with scarlet flowers - a Christmas tree reached to the ceiling on the landing upstairs, reflected in the green lino, with fairy lights and candles, and the excitement as we opened our presents. I remember

Monica, my elder cousin in a beautiful apricot dress I greatly envied. It seems in retrospect that mother did not drink on these occasions and that Christmas was an event quite out of time.

CHAPTER SIX
GREAT SITTING BULL
1928 - 1929

Although I learnt very little at school except to read and write, the fact of leaving the house each day took me out of the closed nightmare of life alone with mother and I enjoyed our maypole dances with the intertwining coloured strands, our games of rounders and nature studies. I made friends and I was the leader of a small gang who trespassed in the grounds of the local big house. We stole roses which, with their thorns removed, could be pushed down the legs of our knickers, paddled in the ornamental ponds and hid in the branches of the chestnut trees. When I was not with the gang I was Mowgli again in the jungle with my beloved companions Baloo the bear and the black panther Bagheera. I still planned to run away to India and sail down the Hooghli and the Ganges and to climb the Himalayas.

My imaginatively enriched life must have in some way affected mother and I sensed unconsciously that I was her only source of love and vitality and that she was pathetically dependent on me for companionship and feared losing me. She still drank as heavily but I was too old now to be knocked about. When she became violent I would either leave the house and go out with my gang, or go to Parsonage Farm. But I began to feel responsible for her and afraid that if I was not there something would happen to her so that if I was away from home she was constantly on my mind. I thought there might be a fire, or that she would get knocked over by a car if she wandered out to look for me. I began to stay with her more or to return home when it was dark. If she was not home when I got back from school I was filled with a terrible anxiety and would go out to look for her, searching the streets and the local woods and lanes. I usually found her and guided her back and she began to believe that we were telepathically in contact and that I must have psychic gifts.

Mother had always been interested in the occult and began to read more about spiritualism and theosophy and she talked a great deal about Annie

Besant and Sir Oliver Lodge and read the Psychic News. I thought this was quite interesting and shared her interest and we would try out some psychic practices. We took it in turns to lie on the wooden top of the bathtub and concentrate on levitation, attempting to rise to the ceiling, but we were not too successful at this nor at table turning. One day mother bought a crystal ball and, still convinced of my psychic gifts, made me gaze into it with her. She would see scenes of violence in which her hated parents came to terrible ends, crashing their Daimler, or going up in flames as Parsonage Farm burnt down. I was frightened and angered by this paranoia and one day stole the crystal ball and dropped it into the River Pinn. I told mother it had been removed by the spirit world because we were misusing it. She was intensely gullible and this mysterious happening increased her belief in my gifts.

I read about automatic writing in the Psychic News so one day I said I would bring her messages from the "other side" and I began writing these for her every evening. I do not remember very clearly the beginnings of this extraordinary period of my life, but from then on when I returned from school I would sit with a pad of lined foolscap paper and a pencil, and pour out messages, eyes tightly shut while the thoughts and advice of Great Sitting Bull and Chief White Buffalo were transmitted through my fertile imagination. It was good that I gave mother such powerful male spirit guardians, thus beginning to safeguard myself from her dependence on my own strength and resilience. I may have learnt about American Indian spirits from reading the Psychic News. I know now that Great Sitting Bull, chief of the Hunkpapa Sioux in the 1830s, was a famous American Indian, war chief, dreamer, mystic and clairvoyant.

I both knew and did not know that I made up these messages, I never planned what I would say but poured out a continual stream of love, advice, support and promises of protection as a parent might have done. I told mother through either Great Sitting Bull or Chief White Buffalo that she was very precious to the spirits on the Other Side and that her life was in their hands, but that she must take better care of her health, smoke less and eat more. The spirits never told her to stop drinking but that she must be careful of her money and pay the milk bill. She could not disobey these instructions and she took them very seriously as they were conveyed with quite remarkable authority. She knew she must obey her spirit guides and as far as I remember she stopped drinking almost at once and her vitality improved miraculously as she felt her world peopled with forces who cared about her. She joined the local spiritualist group and sang happily around the house "Open my eyes that I may see, visions of friends surrounding me" and other cheerful hymns learnt in the group. She cleaned the house, replaced broken gas mantles and the smell of Mansion polish replaced the fumes of tobacco and stale alcohol.

As her health improved I became increasingly depressed. I am sure mother had no inkling of this, since then, under the influence of my Stoic mentor Marcus Aurelius, nothing of my feelings was apparent. But I felt her dependence on me like a great bird of prey squeezing the life out of me. I knew she must be fed, and fed every day with messages of love and hope and I feared the well would one day be dry and I would have no more to give and then she would die. How can I go on satisfying her, I thought? Where will it all end? But Great Sitting Bull and Chief White Buffalo never failed me and the messages continued to pour out night after night, increasing their power over my mother's life. Not only did she clean the house and wash her lovely hair so that it no longer hung lank and smelly, but she began to ask people round to the house for séances and to take me out for meals and for treats to the cinema and to the local tea shop in Pinner High Street.

These treats were marred for me by a deep feeling of pathos, the haunting pity which mars the lives of many children who have to take responsibility for their parents' lives and the dread of the evening ahead when I must bring her messages. I was relieved of the nightmare of her drinking and violence only to fall into another as the dark clouds of guilt engulfed me. I was trapped in my own creation and I believed I was sinning against the Holy Ghost. I had read in the Bible or learnt at Sunday school that it was a sin to commune with the spirits and I knew it was certainly wrong to lie and deceive my mother. My whole life was now built on lies and there was no escape. At Sunday school I had been greatly reassured by the teaching that Jesus cared for children, but now I felt I had lost His love.

I would go for long walks by myself murmuring repeatedly, "Oh what a tangled web we weave, when we first practise to deceive," and I plucked berries from the hedge and ate them with some vague desire to die but nothing happened.

At school I continued to sit at the back of the class, taking nothing in and whenever possible absorbed in the map of India, sailing up the Ganges, walking through the jungle or tramping over the endless plains with the exhausted camels and mules, singing silently to myself to a hymn tune

Kipling's poem:

"Children of the camp are we,
Serving each in his degree,
Children of the yoke and goad,
Pack and harness, pad and load.
We do not know why we or they
March and suffer day by day."

I had imaginary companions, dear Bagheera and the wolf pack, my beloved Wolf Mother and her family, but it was not enough. I was relatively happy at school, but the dread of going home though no longer related to mother's drunkenness was still very heavy with the knowledge of the evening task ahead. For a year I carried this burden of guilt and I saw no end to it.

One morning I was summoned to see the Headmistress of my little school and without any warning I was suddenly exposed. Before then I was hardly aware of being visible in school although I had been attending there for nearly four years. I do not recall any teacher paying special attention to me. I knew I was shunned by children other than my gang because their parents had told them not to have anything to do with me. This shame may not have touched me deeply as it does some children, protected as I was by the dictums of Marcus Aurelius, and my imaginary life in India. With such an inner life why should I bother with the people around me? And as for learning anything, I obviously had fallen so far behind that it was useless to try and understand anything now, but this caused me no concern.

All this was to change. A tall, thin and grubby ten year old I stood sullenly in front of the Headmistress's desk. She looked up from her ledgers and eyed me with distaste. She said "You really are a disgrace - look at your hands and your neck and your filthy blouse". I could not look at my neck but I saw that my hands and arms were indeed ingrained with dirt and my white blouse grey and smelly. I stayed sullen and silent, I had nothing to say and when she asked me why I did not keep myself clean I despised her for not knowing the difficulties. There was no hot water at home, although the copper was heated once a week. The sink was usually full of dirty washing up and we had no iron. I realise now that some children of that age do manage to keep clean and proud of their appearance in equally adverse situations but I suspect they are children with some outside help that balances the neglected conditions at home, or they can go to the home of a relative. I was no longer going to

Parsonage Farm very often as conditions at home had improved and no-one visited us except grandmother once a fortnight. I had nothing to say to the Headmistress, but I was conscious of her strong disapproval. It was as if we came from different worlds. I went back to class, promptly forgot the incident and said nothing about it to mother. But at the end of term she had a letter from father's solicitors enclosing a copy of the school report (which presumably she had seen before but had ignored), in which it was made clear that I was inattentive, bottom of the class, all but illiterate and, more seriously in the eyes of my father probably, failing in moral development. The report stated, no doubt with ample justification, "Joan does not take criticism well" ("Who does?", my analyst commented later) and it went on to comment "She seems sullen and resentful".

My father, about whom I had heard nothing for years, had apparently decided I should go to boarding school and it was assumed under the circumstances mother would agree. She did so with singularly little opposition. She said she would miss me but that she had her spiritualism to comfort her. I decided that now was the time to tell her the truth, that I had made up all the messages. I did this, steeling myself, dreading her reaction and disappointment, but she just laughed and said "No child could have made up such messages". Later she discussed it with grandfather, who agreed with her, and so there it was. They believed I was a gifted medium and I did not worry about it any more. I had confessed and that was all that was required of me and I would give no more messages. The nightmare had ended.

But I wonder if this disbelief, coupled with my fertile imagination, sometimes makes me doubt the veracity of the very careful reports I write for the courts nowadays. I know I am authoritative and convincing and that in reality what I write is a true account of the facts, but perhaps it would have been better for my mental health if I had been exposed as fabricating the spirit writings. I might get less post-report-writing migraine if I had resolved this conflict at the time and had been absolved from spiritual guilt.

Similar conflict has affected telling this story of my life. Although childhood experiences have remained vividly in my mind, I have seldom talked about them except to my analyst and even with her I remained silent and withdrawn for months. Then mother, with whom I had intermittent contact, until she died at the age of 54, once remarked "Well darling, at least you and Peter had happy childhoods to give you a good start in life". It was as if her sad clinging love had completely wiped out the memory of those early years and at the time she said this I was glad of her illusions.

So perhaps I was bound to have a lingering feeling of unreality at times, was it all or in part just a nightmare? It is only in recent years in talking with Ellen, the maid at Rickmansworth, with my cousins and a surviving aunt and most of all with Peter, that I have accepted and felt reassured that my memories are accurate.

CHAPTER SEVEN

THE CONVENT

1930 - 1932

Father decided I should go to a convent in Torquay. He was not a Roman Catholic but Carol, the daughter of one of his great friends, went there and she was doing well. It was arranged that I should spend a week with father to get my uniform, and then be driven to Torquay for the autumn term.

I had not seen father since I was three years of age, and as I only saw him two or three times for short periods before he died, I have no clear memory of him. Peter visited him regularly during the school holidays but I suppose, in accord with the thinking of those times, the 1920s and early 1930s, people thought it was all right for daughters of separated parents to stay all the time with their mothers, and even now the role of fathers in the lives of their daughters is grossly undervalued. But it is strange that I never made any real effort to see him, or he to see me. After mentioning the possibility to my grandfather and being told that if I had anything to do with "the Courts" I would no longer be welcome at the farm, I suppose I had made my choice. But the choice should not have been left to me, and it was, I now think, wicked of grandpa to threaten me with the loss of Parsonage Farm. Sadly children of divorced parents are, I know, frequently exposed to similar forms of moral blackmail and divided loyalties.

I remember staying with father and his housekeeper, Mrs Eleanor Parker, who mother told me was his mistress, in their flat in Gloucester Terrace. I quickly perceived that Mrs Parker was preoccupied and worried about father's health, so I kept out of the way and as quiet as possible. She told me, "He sits for hours in the lavatory and that's always a bad sign". I remember father's concern about the state of my wardrobe and he was very upset when he discovered that I had not been getting the pocket money he sent regularly. I said mother had borrowed it and I felt disloyal to her and sorry for father as obviously this hurt and worried him. I assume that this was because he wanted me to know he cared for me and had not forgotten me.

Mrs Parker took me shopping and I was kitted up with the regulation school uniform, navy skirt, white blouse and tie and initiated into the mysteries of Cash's name tapes, shoe bags, tennis racquet, sponge bag, comb and brushes, all neatly packed away in a new suitcase.

I was driven to Torquay by Uncle Jack, my father's younger brother, whom I disliked on sight. He seemed to me a gloomy character and we said little on this or subsequent journeys. I know now that I reminded him of mother, who, in his view, had ruined father's life. We stopped for lunch at a pub and he brought me out a pie. I was too shy to say I wanted to go to the lavatory and he was too stupid to ask me so I suffered with some discomfort for the whole long journey.

We arrived at Torquay and drove up the long drive to Ilsham and to the convent on the cliffs overlooking fields and sea. A nun came to the door and smiled and said she was Sister Mary. She took us across a long open hall where nuns, with pads on their feet, were polishing the floor, gliding silently backward and forward, their hands hidden in their sleeves, across their bodies, unsmiling, graceful. Sister Mary took me to the lavatory and then into the parlour and said gently, "You must feel like a fish out of water," I nodded, astonished to hear anyone articulate my feelings. I thought it was little short of miraculous that anyone should know how I felt.

Although I was only eleven I was put into a dormitory with the senior girls, six of them. I was tall for my age and perhaps the sisters knew my background and thought I might be too worldly-wise for the younger children. I remember Pat, a fair glamorous girl and Carol, the daughter of my father's friend. I was less interested in people at first than by things and the routine. I had my own locker, a place for my new brush and comb and every Friday there was a neat pile of clean clothes put on the locker in the evening, a clean blouse, socks and pyjamas, navy bloomers, liberty bodice. The bed linen was changed the same day, which was also bath day. A great peace descended on me.

Every morning we went to Mass and to Benediction on Sunday evenings and feast days. I was intoxicated with it all. The incense, the candles, flowers, glorious vestments, the sound of the sanctuary bell. I was enraptured by all the colour and beauty of the Roman Catholic rituals and I spent hours in the chapel worshipping and learning the Stations of the Cross. I must have been starved for colour and music and for aesthetic experience. I bought rosaries and I remember particularly a pale mother of pearl rosary, and holy pictures

I pasted into albums. In chapel I sang "Faith of our fathers" and "Star of the sea" with joy and abandon. It was a time of blissful awakening - the convent was my personal renaissance. My only regret was that as a non-Catholic I could not be a child of Mary and wear the blue ribbon on church parades.

I was put in a class of about twelve other girls of my own age. I did not understand the lessons, though I liked the studious atmosphere and rather wished I could follow what was being taught. But my total ignorance did not go unnoticed as it had in Pinner and soon Sister Mary explained to me that I was going to be put in a class for slightly younger girls so that I could catch up. I sensed that I was expected to be hurt by this but since I had so little understanding of what was expected I was in no way disconcerted, and soon settled happily in the new class sharing a desk with a slightly younger girl called Mary Tew.

She was a Catholic weekly boarder and we soon became inseparable. Together we became besotted by the Lake poets, so much so that I was told on one occasion to hide my flushed excited face behind the desk top until I had calmed down. We were both good at essays and tied for top marks. On school excursions we wandered arm in arm through ruined castles reciting Tennyson, "the splendour falls on castle walls". We were a couple of romantics intoxicated with our first exposure to English literature. Mary, too, was perhaps a little backward scholastically, though less than I was.

When I met her by chance some forty five years later, she had made up for an indifferent educational start and had become a distinguished professor of social anthropology, and the reunion and the reading of her brilliant writings was to inspire me on a new educational voyage late in life studying for a degree at Cambridge. Mary's mother died at the same time as my father so we parted after two years at the convent, and we did not keep in touch.

I suspect that the convent education was quite narrow and the academic standard undemanding. It was a French order and we were supposed to speak French all day. I coped with this by remaining silent or cheating. I doubt if I learnt a great deal in the two years I was there but I was happy. In summer we sat reading and embroidering with Sister Frances under the mulberry tree and occasionally we played a gentle game of tennis. I learnt to swim and after lessons finished, walked over the downs with Mary. We would look for rabbit snares and destroy them - throwing them over the cliffs. Nowadays I carry wire cutters when I go on country walks, but fortunately then we never found a snared rabbit.

One afternoon Sister Mary found me deep in a book, as usual, on the life of a saint. This time it was the life of Sister Theresa, Little Flower. "I would like you to read something else," she said removing the Little Flower gently. She came back with P.C.Wren's "Beau Geste", surely an inspired psychological gesture, balancing my previous absorption in religion. Whatever were her reasons for giving it to me, the book opened up new vistas of romance and adventure. I sometimes think my nature was similar to that of a dried Japanese paper flower which put into water opens up joyously, or like the dormant desert that flowers when the rains come. The convent brought the rain.

Sister Mary was very intuitive and had a great knowledge of her students, but I sensed she sometimes worried about me and about my influence on other pupils. I wondered if she had seen me kiss Mary behind the laurel bush but this only happened on one occasion. I was sexually precocious in mind only at this age. Long since I had countered mother's sexual fantasies with Marie Stopes, but it was true that I thought it was my mission in life to shed scientific knowledge about sex whenever the opportunity arose. I recall carefully explaining about childbirth to my friends, illustrating my instructions with neat drawings of the womb and tubes - I left out the contribution made by the male partner, not I think out of any sense of shame but because it seemed to me to be less interesting.

Taking me aside one day Sister Mary asked me softly, "Do you ever speak or think about things you would be ashamed to share with me?" I was able to answer with absolute truth that I did not and she enquired no further and did not leave me feeling guilty. Indeed she had little cause for concern, and I think she was wise not to probe either into my home life or my feelings, but to just leave me alone to grow and experience the life offered in the safe environment of the blessed convent. I needed that breathing space and I doubt if I could have coped with introspection at this stage, and too much understanding of my circumstances would, I think, have been overwhelming. I needed an experience of normal childhood and of having adults responsible for organising the day and bringing order to chaos. I was entirely confident in the wisdom of the established order. I did not even question the revolting food which consisted mainly of watery marrow on toast, if I recall rightly, and crabmeat. With kindly masochism I would eat my neighbour's portion too if she could not as we were required to clear our plates.

And so the ordered days passed and I learnt to do simple fractions and to play scales on the piano and Sister Mary told me, "I expect great things from you one day, Joan". I treasured these words and did not know until I met Mary Tew forty-five years later that she had said the same thing to her, and probably to all her pupils, but no matter. They made an indelible impression on me, and Sister Mary joined my inner mentors and would continue to influence my life though we never met again after I left the convent. I think it may have been those two years and the first settled years of infancy that laid down a pattern in my psyche, so that I am inclined to think it is time to change course every two or three years. I feel restless and want to move on and go walkabout. In the summer of 1932, at the age of thirteen, my childhood ended, as did my formal education.

CHAPTER EIGHT

MY FATHER'S DEATH

1932

For whom do they mourn
The black funereal horses
Tossing their plumed heads in dark affray?
Black on black their plumes shut out the day.

I who did not share the mourning
Now hear their hooves ring out the empty dawn.

Joan Court

That summer of 1932 I spent half the school holidays with father and his family in Maidenhead in their house by the river. Peter had always spent some of his holidays there and said he found the contrast quite uncanny: on the one hand the misery and sordid surroundings of Pinner, and on the other hand the comfort and elegance of summer days on the river with regattas, cleaning out the punts, being dressed in spotless white on Sundays, calling out to his friends on other boats, and visiting the lovely houses with lawns down to the river. I had never stayed in Maidenhead before and I found the atmosphere quite repressive, perhaps because, though I did not know it then, father was depressed. I remember very little of my paternal grandfather, other than he looked rather like a dried out mandarin as he sat at table, and neither he nor grandmother took much notice of me. I expect they found me a quiet and difficult child too, unlike my brother who was more extrovert and a better mixer.

I remember father coming into my room one evening and giving me a new copy of "The Jungle Book" and of "Cricket on the Hearth", and I would lie in bed reading and listening to the comforting sound of trains in the distance.

One evening he came into my room and tried to explain to me why the separation from mother had taken place. I understood that he did not want me to blame him or think he did not care for me, but on the other hand he would not say anything against mother. I did not know how to reassure him or make him feel less sad, though in fact it had never occurred to me to blame him in any way as I had not believed my mother's accounts of his failings. But I had spent so little time with him. I had not seen him in the eight years after he left home so I did not know how to respond, and though I wanted to be near him I felt rather embarrassed.

On the day I was to return to Pinner I went with his mother and his brother Jack to see him off from Maidenhead station to London. As the train steamed out, tears poured down my face silently, I could not stop weeping and grandma said, "The child should never have come." I do not remember weeping for him ever again, at least not until many years later. But I think the separation from him and his death is the major tragedy of my life, far more than mother's drinking.

I returned to Pinner. It was extremely hot and indeed the newspapers of that period report that in August the temperature soared into the 80s and 90s day after day. On August 19th I was sitting with mother in the early evening under the elderberry tree and the air was still and oppressive, I was reading a book, and mother the Evening News. Suddenly she made a shocked sound and thrust the paper towards me saying "Your father is dead," and I saw the headline on the front page: "Eminent solicitor falls to death from window of London hotel."

I went to fetch Peter who was with friends up the road. "Keep calm," he said, but indeed I was in no danger of showing any panic or feeling because I felt nothing.

I have wiped out the memory of subsequent events - I know we did not go to the funeral and it was not until about thirty years or so later when I checked the actual newspaper accounts, that I found that father had left a note referring to us children. "I hope my children make a better success of their lives than I have done." At the time the reasons for his suicide were explained by mother as being due to debts and she said that he had a woman with him in the hotel and that he had quarrelled with her. I cannot imagine where these fantasies came from as the truth was quite otherwise, as I discovered when I checked the newspapers at the British Museum. The Coroner recorded a verdict of suicide whilst of unsound mind, and said that father's real trouble was ill health and that he was affected by the intense heat. He commented that "Mr. Court's affairs were in perfect order. Although separated from his wife this was an arrangement of longstanding. He was a temperate man and had no troubles other than ill health brought on by the heat and recent illness". He was only forty.

I feel a sense of great respect for the manner of his death and the way he set about doing it with the intention of being no trouble to anyone - booking into a hotel and making sure his work at the office and his other affairs were "in perfect order". I only wish that we had seen then the note he left for us as it would have been something we would have treasured all our childhood. I am conscious that his intentions were moral - he did not want to be a burden to anyone, and felt that if he could not work then he would be. It is also typical for such a pedantic character to bungle the carefully thought out plan when it came to action. He had intended to end his life by cutting his arteries and bleeding to death in the bath. The Coroner's report says "There was an opened blood-stained razor found on the bathroom floor and the water in the bath was blood-stained and he had injuries on his wrist and thigh." But when this attempt failed he locked the bathroom door from the outside, no doubt hoping to stop the chamber-maid being shocked, and then jumped out of the window. He must have been desperate because he was only wearing his slippers and for a modest man not to have put on his dressing gown shows a profound degree of mental disorder. He fell on railing spikes which pierced him before he fell into the area ten feet below pavement level. He was still conscious when he was discovered by the night watchman but died in the ambulance on the way to St. Mary's, Paddington. Although he was said to be conscious, the fact that he had fallen eighty-five feet makes me wonder how much he really knew.

I never saw any of the Court family again until very many years later when I visited his brother Jack in the solicitors' firm. I wish now I had made more attempt to meet people of my father's generation so I could have learnt more about him.

After his death there seemed to be no money although it could well be that mother did not mention that she had an allowance for us and I did not check father's will until much later. Our grandfather arranged for Peter to leave his public school and start an apprenticeship in engineering, and it was assumed that I would stay with mother, "Now you are all I've got," she said ominously. Mother must have decided that she and I should go to work. But how it came about that we found jobs and left Peter alone in Pinner, I cannot imagine. He told me later that he found himself lodgings with a pleasant family in Pinner, where he stayed until he had completed his engineering training. We then lost touch for many years. When he had nearly completed his training grandpa told him that as he had given him a good training and that it would soon be finished he would then give him £5 and he would be on his own. Peter's chief Mechanical Engineer wanted to send him to the Bolivia and Antofagasta Railway, but Peter just walked into the offices of the Empire of India and Ceylon Tea Company and asked to go to India. In three weeks he was on his way, having called at grandpa's office before and told him that he would not need his £5!

It is sad that Peter and I lost touch with each other for many years and only saw each other or communicated sporadically. This is the case with many children from sad families, it is as if they want no reminders of the time of their childhood together.

CHAPTER NINE

DOMESTIC SERVICE

1932 - 1934

Mother had never worked outside the home, but she was very enterprising and perhaps being widowed gave her a new lease of life. She started reading advertisements in "The Lady" and looking for jobs for us both. Although I was not quite fourteen I looked at least fifteen, which was school leaving age then and there was no question of my returning to the convent. Passive recipient of nature's fortune, I never raised the possibility. Mother responded to an advertisement for "Mother's Helps" to take over the domestic duties on a remote Cornish farm. "One to cook and the other to do the housework. Live as family." I do not remember the interview, nor the move, nor the fact that we left Peter alone in the house, but I recall arriving at the Helford River in Cornwall and the farm on the cliff edge. Although mother did not cook much when we were children she did know how to boil vegetables, make tea and toast and she would sometimes roast a joint. But it is amazing that she was able to cook for seven adults, or at least help with the cooking in the Cornish family especially as all the cooking was done under very primitive conditions on stinking oil and primus stoves.

The family consisted of the farmer and his wife and their two sons and I have vague memories of the wife being quite congenial, but of not making any particular relationship with her or the family. There was also a daughter of my own age away at boarding school and there were sundry beautiful dogs and farm cats. We ate with the family and my keenest memories were of lovely bowls of clotted cream at every meal. I did not find the housework particularly arduous and I quite liked cleaning and washing up and bringing order. I had some experience of this as during school holidays I had little cleaning jobs in Harrow biking over to a smart suburban house full of brass from India which I polished with reverent care, so I had some idea of how to set about the tasks at the farm.

In Cornwall I had a half day off a week on a different day from mother and I bought a bicycle which at more than one time in my life has been a passport to freedom, next best thing to a horse. I cycled into Falmouth, or swam in the river, or walked by it on long excursions through that lovely hydrangea-scented landscape. The sea and woods were all around and often I would bike back in the dark at night after a long afternoon in the country intoxicated with it all as the owls hooted me home.

I do not remember being at all unhappy or lonely, though when the daughter of the house came home for holidays I was conscious of some dim resentment. We hardly exchanged a word and I imagined there was social distance between us because of our different status. We lived "with the family" but our tasks were menial and though of course I knew we were "gentlewomen" this may not have been apparent to the untutored eye! My resentment, hardly that, really more of a quiet envy, was because the girl was at school and my two years in the convent had done nothing to disillusion me about what I perceived as the idyllic life of girls' boarding schools, illusions which cause my young friends now to give forth hollow laughs. To me then my imagination, coloured more by fiction than the convent, was of best friends, arms linked, sharing secrets, midnight feasts, excursions to the haunted castle, the romance of the head girl, of laughter, warmth and caring teachers urging this bright girl (surely it must be me?) to work hard at her classics studies and gain a scholarship to university. Not that I had a clue then what a university was.

Sister Mary wrote to me, and I remember her letter clearly, her condolence for my father's death, her regret that I had to leave, "just as you were beginning to catch up," and I know I felt sad about this. But I was so accustomed to putting my feelings aside and getting on with the next task that I do not really know what I felt about it. I do remember watching the crocodiles of girls from the Falmouth schools on their walks with great longing and hanging about school playing fields absorbed in the girls' netball and cricket matches. So began, I think, the life-long search for education and my delight in learning anything new. I often think that people in the western world have little concept now of this hunger for learning which spurs on children and adults who have not had education as a right. One has only to see the little children in remote Indian villages trudging their way, swinging their tiffin carrier with its frugal lunch miles across the paddy fields to school, to know about this.

Apart from these feelings and my love of the beautiful countryside, little of note happened to me in Cornwall other than a significant experience as a hospital patient which may have touched the first chord of a vocation in nursing. I did the washing up at the farm in a large wooden tub and I got a splinter under a thumb nail. This went septic and mother advised me to put on a bread poultice. I did this but the thumb became very painful and I saw pus gathering under the nail. So on my next half day without mentioning my intention to mother or the family I went to the casualty department of Falmouth Hospital. There was some consternation about the state of my thumb and hand, as by then the infection had spread upwards and I was told to come back the next day for admission. Meanwhile a kaolin poultice was applied and my arm put in a sling. Next day I was driven to the hospital by my employers, and admitted. The nail was removed under anaesthetic and the pus drained off. I felt quite confident in the hospital care and when I woke up in the ward watched all that was going on with great interest. Here was drama, efficiency making people better, all within what I perceived as an ordered and informed routine similar to the convent. I talked to the staff nurse and said that I would like to be a nurse one day. She was kind to me but made some puzzling comment that I might have some difficulty gaining admission for training. She meant because I was in domestic service and I noted this reservation without giving it much weight. I simply put the idea aside for a time, instinctively knowing that ideas and plans germinate in their own way.

Soon after my fourteenth birthday mother decided that we should move on. I think our work was satisfactory, so I do not know why we moved but I did not object. I have no memory of the mechanics of the change, but felt rather sad about leaving the animals and the sea and the beautiful cliff walks.

Once again mother scanned "The Lady" and answered an advertisement from an army family in Aldershot for mother and daughter to cook and clean, not this time "as family" but the advertisement did specify "Two gentlewomen - mother and daughter or friends." Mother cleverly arranged for the interview to take place at Parsonage Farm where we went to stay for a short while between jobs, so once again I could renew my love affair with the house and garden. It was as it always was - high summer with great peaches ripening on the kitchen garden wall, fat gooseberries on the bushes where in our early years Peter and I had spent long lovely afternoons plucking them. There were great bowls of redcurrants in the house. Parsons was still bent over his flower pots while his cat wound herself round or stalked amongst the plants. We had tea on the lawn under the cedar tree, as always, cucumber sandwiches, coffee cake from Fuller's and tea in the silver teapot. Out in the yard the chickens pecked and in the morning I woke with the cock crowing and the bark of the Clumber dogs. It was as it always was. If it ever rained I do not remember it.

Major and Mrs. Nancy Yates came to interview us and I am sure mother felt quite gleeful at their barely suppressed astonishment at the setting - a proper show-off really, but clever of mother to arrange it so, as if it were the most natural thing in the world. We were taken on, so I assume our references from Cornwall were in order, and shortly after the interview we set out for Aldershot. The army quarters were some miles out, and set near to woods. The Yates had a little girl, Susan, aged about three and a beautiful Alsatian bitch with whom I fell instantly in love - Mother Wolf, of course, straight from "The Jungle Book". This began a very happy period for me and we stayed there, I think, for about nine months. I grew devoted to Nancy Yates, the first of a series of mother figures and she responded to my devotion with tact and wisdom, helping me to begin to gain some emotional distance from mother who was very possessive, as indeed she had always been, hating my friends and casting a cloud over all relationships. I was afraid of her jealousy and even as a young child I tried to keep my friendships to myself.

Nancy was worried about her little girl who seemed too quiet and repressed in the care of the Norland nanny. After I had been there for some months she dismissed the nanny and asked me to look after Susan, and we shared the work of the house and the child care. I took Susan out on long expeditions on her pony with the Alsatian dancing beside us, and the child quickly responded to the freedom and cast aside her unnatural goodness. I remember peaceful afternoons with the child or learning some skill from Nancy who taught me how to lay the table for dinner and clean the silver and make real mayonnaise. In the mornings I made the beds and cleaned around. In Nancy's room I would bury my face in her fur coat in an ecstasy of delight at its warmth and her perfume.

On my half day I enrolled in typing classes in Aldershot. I never told mother about this as I was learning to be very secretive. My greatest ambition was to go up in an aeroplane on a pleasure flight advertised as costing half-a-crown for half an hour in the air. I did ask mother about this and she emphatically refused permission, thinking no doubt that it was dangerous. Nancy knew of this ambition, perceived that it had some symbolic significance to me, a gesture of independence perhaps, and she encouraged me to rebel, casting no doubt on the rightness of this ambition. So on one of my half days I went to the airfield and booked a flight and up we went, up and up, in a Gypsy Moth plane. I remember that it was open and the pilot looked back at my exhilarated expression and promptly looped the loop. The world turned upside down and my stomach lurched into my head. Down below the little fields were all patchwork and like my beloved toy farm with lead fences and two dimensional oak trees. I felt a great love for the world, for the sky and for life itself. It was a flight in more senses than one and I took a psychic leap into a new freedom. It marked a stand against my mother. She could hardly claim obedience from me now since I had been self supporting for over a year, but we shared a room and our relationship continued to be stifling. I knew she was jealous of Nancy and my childlike devotion to her, sensing in it an emotional attachment in which she played no part. Nancy herself, I knew, cared about me, though not necessarily for me and she was the first ordinary, normal, maternal woman to whom I had been close. Sister Mary was a model too, but as a nun she belonged literally to a different order of things. Nancy was a family person with her own settled life and child and I had not been in contact with ordinary family life before.

Shortly after the flight I had shocking evidence of the depths of my murderous hatred of mother. She was in bed, I remember, and I do not know what started off our quarrel, since we seldom quarrelled, though she had always taunted me about my relationships. She must have said something about Nancy. I was brushing my hair before getting into bed, and probably looking indifferent and withdrawn. Something must have goaded her into a sudden frenzy of jealousy because she made a comment which I now cannot remember, but it was to do with lesbianism. I understood what she meant. This was still the 1930s and long before the days of sexual liberation. Any deviation was regarded as grossly abnormal. But whatever it was she said I was suddenly impelled into a murderous rage and the shades of Marcus Aurelius were for a split second cast aside! I cannot remember losing my temper before or since. I was across the room and had my hands around her throat and choked her. She fended me off but what brought me to my senses was not her physical defence but the fear in her eyes. It was all over in an instant and we must have made it up, or more likely mother would have pretended that it never happened, but she made no more comments about my love for Nancy.

It was quite soon after this episode, but perhaps there is no connection, that mother began talking of us going overseas. It could have been no life for her in Cornwall or Aldershot and although I am inclined to forget it, she was a beautiful woman still in her early thirties and no doubt wanted more out of life now she was widowed. I wish I could describe her in more detail but it seems to me that we had so little in common and I had suffered so much at her hands that I could not and cannot perceive her as a person in her own right. Reading some of her letters now I can see she was alert and intelligent and many people have referred to her beauty.

I was now fifteen and could see that emigrating would be a great adventure. I would have preferred to go to India, and mother looked into that possibility. But the people with whom we dealt, agents of a voluntary organisation called The Society for the Overseas Settlement of British Women offered us the opportunity to go to Cape Town. They paid the passage and were responsible for meeting us there and finding us jobs. We were asked to wear a purple rosette when we landed and these we carefully put away in our bags. We embarked in the spring and were seen off by the Yates's. Nancy had made me a charming rose coloured evening dress with a lace collar for dinners on board. I did not see Nancy or Susan again.

CHAPTER TEN

CAPE TOWN

1934 - 1936

We sailed from Southampton on a Union Castle boat, the Grantully Castle; surely almost her last voyage as she was not in her first youth or beauty. I read that in 1892 she was once lent by her owner to Mr. Gladstone so that he could restore his health with a sea voyage. The boat was packed with Jewish refugees from Germany. I knew nothing about Nazism, or indeed about Europe - I never read a newspaper and world events had no meaning for me. It is quite hard really for anyone to appreciate the depth of my ignorance. All that I learnt in subsequent years right up to the time I went to university in my late thirties was picked up at random and from contact with well informed people. My inner life was nurtured not by the world of reality but from books and poetry, and I was abysmally ignorant of world events.

On the voyage we stopped at Madeira, and I deliberately got drunk to see how it felt. I was tenderly returned to my bunk by Gerhardt, a gentle non-Jewish boy who protected my innocence and taught me to play chess. He tried to explain to me about conditions in Germany. I understood that he could no longer see his Jewish girlfriend, and I began to have some inkling of racial prejudice. Gerhardt was pleased to see that I talked to the lonely black South African travelling by himself in the steerage. It would not have occurred to me to do otherwise as this was one thing I had learnt from mother, who, although a snob by any standards, was quite without colour or racial prejudice.

The voyage was beautiful and I spent hours watching the flying fish and phosphorescence in the wake of our ship, and lying at night on deck under the stars watching the sky swaying peacefully as the band played "When the Blue of the Night Meets the Gold of the Day", and "Night and Day, You are the One".

I did not know how to dance and tended to repel the advances of the leering men from First Class, who would occasionally come on the Second Class deck. I was content with the gentle friendship of Gerhardt who explained to me that I might prefer him to be a real aggressive lover, but that he felt protective towards me. He would carefully move another pawn on our chessboard and fetch me an orange juice.

Mother and I shared a cabin with a South African lady returning to her family after a visit "home". I thought her very worldly and remember her comment about my figure when I was undressing, "with a figure like that you could be an artist's model." I carefully filed this observation in my mental holdall for future reference. I was not sure what it meant, but I was sure that one day it might come in useful.

The voyage took three weeks and we stopped at Lobito Bay where it was exceedingly hot and we went through the initiation rituals of crossing the Equator, throwing each other into the swimming pool. At dawn three weeks later we docked in the beautiful Cape of Good Hope harbour with Table Mountain cutting the sky and beyond that all of Africa. We were met wearing our purple ribbons and after a brief stay in a hostel run by the Organisation we were placed together on a farm where I "helped out" and mother cooked. I remember the wonderful fruit and sunshine, the smell of melons and the rich earth, of arum lilies up Table Mountain where I climbed on my days off, the firs and the oaks, the magnolias and the gardens full of purple broom and geraniums and carpets of flowers. Once I climbed up Kloof Nek and saw a great sailing ship coming into the harbour. It must have been taking part in a grain race.

I do not know how it came about, but I managed to convince mother and the Organisation that I ought to have different work and "get on" because I soon found myself another job. This time out of housework and into unskilled office work in a convent up Kloof Nek. I was the porteress and dealt with visitors to the orphanage. There were about a hundred little "coloured" children, as they were then called, and for a time I was asked to help with them. I was ashamed to find that I could not control them and after one of the nuns found quite a riot going on at bedtime I was removed from this duty and returned to the porteress lodge to help Mrs. Heseltine, the convent secretary. She was good to me, teaching me office routine and how to bleach my hair with camomile leaves. I liked being taken in hand. One of my jobs was to act as messenger to the Bishop and I enjoyed these trips down the hill in the sunshine, buying grapes on the way there and back and spitting out the pips.

I gloried in the sun and sky and on my half days I went swimming and drank iced coffee in a cafe off Adelaide Street.

At this time my inner life was nurtured reading the Indian poets, in particular the work of the Nobel Prize winner, the Bengali poet Rabindranath Tagore. I read "Gitanjali" and longed both to go to Bengal and to write poetry. Books had been and always would be my lifeline so it was natural I thought the art of writing the most desirable thing in the world. I reasoned that I would not become a writer unless I had a typewriter, but I could not afford to buy one on my wage. I recalled the comment about my figure made on the voyage, and so went to the University Arts School and asked the Principal if a model was needed. There was a vacancy, and he asked me to strip and walk about. I did this and after a quick glance I was engaged. Looking back it seems to me that I exhibited quite extraordinary determination and nerve and absence of modesty, but then I was so intent on getting a typewriter come what may. Modelling must surely be one of the most exhausting and boring jobs one can do, and I cannot agree with Quentin Crisp's views that it is an interesting and simple way to earn money. I remember the first moment of alarm when stepping out naked from behind the screen I was told how to stand and instantly about twenty pencils went up in front of me from the class. After this there were no further alarms and I rested for five minutes every half an hour and collected my five shillings for each session. I soon had my typewriter and practised the touch typing I had begun to learn in Aldershot.

I do not remember much about the convent regime, though I was impressed by the Reverend Mother, an ascetic, tall woman who occasionally gave me a bleak smile. The bookshelves in her room were full of novels and detective stories and I felt she had a strong inner life in the world as well as in her community.

I was now nearly sixteen, a tall, strong young woman with fair (bleached) hair and I was conscious of romantic feelings but I never met any young people and I did not know how to mix with them, so I had no social life outside the convent. I did not dream of marrying and having children but then I never read women's magazines and had no model in my own life of what a normal family pattern might be.

One day on the way to lunch I saw a topee on the table outside the office and learnt that a girl had arrived from Scotland, a relative of one of the nuns, to spend some time in Cape Town to broaden her mind. I met Jane at lunch, she was tall and willowy, with long brown hair neatly harpooned in a severe bun at the nape of her neck, in her early twenties, wearing a lady-like cream linen suit and no make up. I was unclear what her plans were for the future, but there she was and propinquity is all when one is love-starved and romantic.

Jane had no friends in Cape Town so I had the welcome task of showing her round. We went for picnics up Table Mountain and drank grape juice in Adelaide Street and I would buy her flowers off the street market. She did not swim when we went to Simons Bay but sat contentedly on the beach watching me in the water, and we sat under the pine trees up Kloof Nek reading and writing and sharing our thoughts. She was the first young friend I had made since I left the convent and I was soon passionately in love with her and longed above all to release her long hair and touch her breasts. I showed her the romantic poetry typed with such feverish haste on my new typewriter and in the late evening would find any excuse to visit her room. I cannot imagine what the poor girl made of all this. She was, I think, both alarmed and intrigued. As my knowledge of sexual matters had all been gleaned from the works of Marie Stopes, who gave no instruction in the art of love between women, my relationship with Jane did not bring complete sexual fulfilment but it was my first intimate relationship and aroused in me great passion and joy not untinged with guilt.

The relationship could not have gone unnoticed in the convent but no comments were made and the sun-filled days continued. Jane spent a great deal of her time in the Porteress Room where I sat doing some simple office tasks for Mrs Heseltine and she would come with me when I went on my errands down town or to the Post Office. In the evenings we would go for walks or sit together under the magnolia tree in the convent courtyard. We longed for my half day so that we could roam further a field and in the evenings we made love in our artless way.

The months went by and suddenly one morning the Mother Superior summoned me to her room and my heart sank with guilt and dread which increased with her opening words, "Joan, I am concerned that you may be getting too tired," as I thought this must refer to the time I was spending with Jane or to my job as an artist's model. I had never discussed my modelling job with her, but I guessed she must have talked to Mrs. Heseltine about it. Mother Superior was not apparently worried about the possibility of moral danger and she was quite right, there was none. The students, if one ever met them at the end of a session, were formal and polite and modelling for a class does not appear to encourage eroticism.

Mother Superior wanted to talk about her concern for Jane who she felt had no purpose in life, and she hoped I might infuse her with some of my own zest and decisiveness, or words to that effect. I was astonished and did not know how to respond. Mother Superior's next comment came as a bombshell, she wondered if I had ever thought about a career? I hardly knew what a career was but it did not matter as Mother Superior proceeded to tell me what she had in mind for me. She wondered if I would be interested in training in South Africa as a nursery nurse, but quickly sensing that this had little appeal (I reminded her that I could not even control a small dormitory of children going to bed), she then went on to talk about her next option. She thought I should go back to England and not waste any more time in Cape Town and train as a hospital nurse. "You must go to St. Thomas'," she said, "It's the best hospital in the world and the training there would mean you could travel anywhere in the world once you were qualified. I shall cable your grandfather for the money for your passage," she went on, "and you must tell your mother what is planned. I would like you to sail on the Winchester Castle which leaves on March 12th." As it was now mid-February I was once again impelled into a new life with considerable speed, but this time I do remember the actual departure and the terrible anxiety I had about telling mother of the plan.

I left this until the last week as I could not bear to hurt her, and there was no way of softening the blow. She was indeed dreadfully upset, although by now she had a life of her own in Cape Town and we had seen very little of each other. Although I hated telling her I also felt a great wave of relief and freedom at the thought of leaving her in South Africa and being on my own as I still felt her dependency like an albatross about my neck.

Then there was the heartbreak of leaving Jane, although she perhaps was quite relieved in some ways at the prospect of our separation since her ardour had always been much short of my own, but I could not imagine how I would live without her and said that I would write to her every day. Unfortunately I had to leave my typewriter as I had not paid off all the instalments. Sadly and reluctantly I gave it back to the shop, and it was many years before I had another. But otherwise, complete with tin trunk and bags I took myself to the dock, for some reason unaccompanied, but helped by a kindly black porter, who refused to take a tip, to my berth on the Winchester Castle. Grandpa had sent the fare - £28 - and I had saved some pocket money for the voyage.

I felt dreadfully grieved at leaving Jane as I suspected I would never see her again, and indeed this was true. She wrote later to say that "our relationship will distract you from a greater interest" whatever that might mean. She said she felt she should not be the focus for such energy and passion, but all through the voyage and for many months afterwards I continued to pour out my heart in letters quoting at length from the poems of Ella Wheeler-Wilcox and Christina Rosetti.

On the boat I had a protector in an enormous Grenadier Guard, nicknamed Tiny. As there were so few girls on board I suppose he felt it worthwhile spending his time sitting beside me in the deckchair. Although I was nearly seventeen, I was emotionally immature and took no pride in my appearance. I was beginning to look quite stodgy; healthy and robust no doubt but hardly physically attractive. Years of hiding emotion had drained away any natural vivacity and I think of myself then, and to some extent now, as lacking in facial expression. "You've got such a wooden face," my mother used to say with some truth and I developed this perverted pride in not showing my feelings. My curious upbringing had deprived me of the social skills needed to relate to men, at least in the flirtatious way appropriate to those times, but I felt grateful to Tiny particularly in the Bay of Biscay when we ran into bad weather and he refused to allow me to be sea-sick, saying it was all in the mind, and marching me smartly round the deck booming out rousing military songs and, when these ran out, strengthening, morale-boosting hymns. So roaring "Onward Christian Soldiers" we challenged the rough seas and kept sickness at bay.

CHAPTER ELEVEN

A NIGHTINGALE NURSE

1936 - 1938

Back at Parsonage Farm grandmother noted how bleached my hair was from the South African sun and of course I said nothing about Mrs Heseltine's improving camomile rinses. I did tell grandfather about Tiny, as he had invited me to go to London and have an evening with him in the barracks. Grandfather, responding moderately and hiding his shock, said that I was still too young to meet a man on my own, but that I could ask him again when I was eighteen. As I was only just seventeen this could have meant a long wait had I cared either way, but I was glad of an excuse to turn down the invitation.

I had discovered that my grandparents thought I must be pregnant or in some other dire distress for Mother Superior to cable for my passage money home and I think they were rather put out to find no such drama emerging. Unfortunately Mother Superior had neglected to follow up her cable with an explanatory letter. When I told my grandparents about the suggestion of training as a nurse, they had some doubts as they considered it a rough life for a lady, "You will meet all sorts and types, mostly unsavoury," said grandfather, but he said he would help me if that was my choice. On the other hand he did not feel it sensible for me to apply to St. Thomas' as this was obviously the most élite establishment, and that I had better begin in Watford or some other local training school. I listened politely and then sent off a letter of enquiry to St. Thomas' Hospital. I knew that Mother Superior's advice was the best and intended to follow it unswervingly. When a reply came from Matron's office signed by Dame Alicia Lloyd, grandfather was quite impressed and wrote a supportive letter on headed paper. "Always go to the top," he said rather inconsistently.

In due course I was interviewed by Dame Alicia, now a legendary figure in the history of that great training school. She looked at me closely and said, "I am not entirely satisfied with your education, but you look the right sort." In those days it was possible to get into St. Thomas' if you appeared to have a vocation, good health, came from a professional family and, apparently, "looked the right sort". Good health was actually last on the list and the death rate for nurses from tuberculosis was quite high. The girls from professional families normally had a good education and Dame Alicia did not enquire closely into why I had not completed my schooling. Perhaps she did not like to trouble me, knowing from my application of my father's early death. She said I was much too young to begin training. Probationers were not admitted then until they were twenty-one, but for some reason an exception was made in my case, and subsequently I believe with other nurses, and it was agreed that I might start training when I was nineteen. Meanwhile she ordered that I should go to a pre-nursing establishment in Bristol - St. Monica's Home of Rest - where I could learn some practical skills and prepare to take the Entrance Examination of the General Nursing Council which consisted of a general knowledge paper, an essay and a simple maths paper for applicants who had not obtained the Cambridge Certificate and Matriculation usually required of entrants.

St. Monica's is a large complex of buildings set in its own grounds on Clifton Common on the outskirts of Bristol. The patients, all women, were middle-aged or elderly and suffering from some form of chronic disorder. There were many ex-missionaries and they were cared for by a sprinkling of trained nurses helped by young women like myself waiting to take up a career in nursing. We learnt simple nursing tasks and had elementary lectures in hygiene, anatomy and physiology. The atmosphere was genteel, religious and unexciting but I settled into the routine in my usual uncritical way and made friends with the other girls with whom I went on lengthy biking expeditions when we were off duty. I still wrote to Jane but soon she became dream-like in my imagination and slipped away from my mind. I did not have any passionate friendships at St. Monica's, though I remember a passing affair which was more sexual than loving. This has stayed in my mind because of the aplomb with which another girl coming into my bedroom without knocking said, "I'm so sorry I did not know you were resting" on finding me lying on the bed with another girl, both of us naked and no doubt looking very guilty.

The two years passed uneventfully and soon it was time to take the General Nursing Council Entrance Exam. I must have done well enough although I remember with some shame that I wrote that Sarah Bernhardt was a scientist in the multi-choice section. I then wrote to St. Thomas' reminding them that

I had been offered a vacancy if I completed the two years and passed the examination. This was not quite true but Dame Alicia Lloyd had left by then and perhaps the notes on my original application were not clear, for in fact I had not been given a conditional vacancy. I was accepted and left St. Monica's in March 1938 ready to take up the vacancy in St. Thomas' in May.

I had not been able to save any money on the pittance we earned at St. Monica's and I wondered if there was any charitable fund available to enable me to buy the uniform and other items needed for entrance into the Nightingale School in St. Thomas'. Nothing if not resourceful, I found the Solicitors Benevolent Fund listed in a charity book and wrote to them explaining my needs. I was interviewed and granted a lump sum immediately and a small allowance to be paid quarterly throughout my training. The secretary who interviewed me told me that had I applied earlier the Fund would have probably paid for my continued education through to university. I felt desolate about the missed opportunity because I was increasingly aware of my lack of formal education and an ardent desire to learn. My handwriting was atrocious and my spelling worse. I had no basic knowledge of mathematics and few cultural interests. I had, though, begun to be interested in Indian politics, following the Indians' fight for independence and Mahatma Gandhi's non-violent tactics mostly through the writings of Kingsley Martin in the "New Statesman." This led me to read books and articles written by the Mahatma and books about him and I was soon converted to pacifism and vegetarianism and thus already marked as a social deviant.

Walking across Westminster Bridge to St. Thomas' on the first day, I looked at the eight great blocks of the hospital and wondered what it all held for me, but I was more conscious of the weight of my large cheap suitcase. I could not afford a taxi and arrived at Riddell House, the Nurses Home, somewhat out of breath. Other new entrants were arriving and we were told to go to our rooms and change into uniform. Easier said than done. My stiff collar was much too big and I had forgotten to buy studs for the belt and collars. I was rescued by another girl and then in our new attire we gathered in the classroom to be given initial instructions and time sheets. We would be in the preliminary training school for three months and then if our work was satisfactory we would begin our probationary year in the Nightingale Home before becoming staff nurses at the end of this period. Florence Nightingale, who founded St. Thomas' Hospital Nursing School, believed that it only took one year to train a nurse to take responsibility, so although our training was for four years we were expected to take on considerable responsibility after the first year and there was a clear demarcation between the first and subsequent years - both in our uniforms and in the way we were regarded. Our uniform was very elaborate compared to the skimpy school-girl type dresses worn by modern nurses and we were encouraged to take immense pride in our appearance. Our caps were spotted muslin goffered elaborately and oval-shaped when first laundered. These had to be stitched up and then perched on our heads and pinned with a butterfly effect over our buns. We were all expected to have long hair and if we were still at the stage of growing it we wore a "disgrace cap" until it was long enough to be rolled up and the cap firmly pinned in place. At the outbreak of war, eighteen months later, we all had to cut off our hair for fear of spreading typhus.

I managed to hold my own in the preliminary training school much helped by a kind fellow student of my own set who sat beside me in lectures and helped me out when I got stuck with spelling or comprehension. There were seventeen of us in the set, about half of whom completed the training. I found the practical side of the instructions harder than the theory, and indeed it is a mystery to me how I ever managed to become a nurse as I am quite deficient in manual ability. We were taught the most intricate bandaging, and mine invariably came off or were too loose and it took me weeks to make a padded splint. I coped with the invalid cooking and learned to make a wine jelly. I was terribly anxious to get everything right and continued to be plagued with fear of failure or not pleasing my seniors all through training. I had fewer doubts about pleasing the patients.

Towards the end of the preliminary training school time we were sent to the wards for a few hours daily. These were on the Nightingale model - that is fifteen beds to each side and sometimes with extra beds put at the end of the ward or in the middle, with sluices and bathrooms on either side. The wards all overlooked the Thames and the Houses of Parliament and there were balconies on which those in the medical wards suffering from tuberculosis were nursed. In the centre of the ward were the sinks and a table on which stood a splendid copper urn full of boiling water. Later on night duty I learnt that it could be adjusted so as to make the finest drip coffee. The medicine cupboard was near to the door and through this was the kitchen and the Sister's room and the great clanging lifts in which we ferried our patients to x-rays and theatre.

My first ward was a surgical one. We called the Sisters by the names of their wards, and I think my first encounter with one of these beings, in her elegant navy and white spotted dress, was Sister Nuffield. Sisters were immensely impressive, as were the charge nurses, trained Nightingales who deputised for Sister when she was off duty. Both Sister and charge nurses seemed light years away from probationer nurses but I was probably more intimidated than most young women as I took the whole experience with intense seriousness. I was very upset indeed when I got a most indifferent report from my first ward placement due, I think, partly to general incompetence, but also because Sister took a poor view of me because she thought I was "blood-thirsty". I had expressed enthusiasm to accompany a patient to the theatre, instead of waiting my turn. I did this because I was scared stiff and thought I had better get it over with and take the plunge as soon as possible, but how was Sister to know? As it was, I fainted in the theatre and continued to do so whenever I had theatre duty.

This poor report resulted in me being sent for by Matron. Dame Alicia had left by now and the new matron addressed me sadly saying she knew how difficult it was for young girls to give up their freedom, their dances and the cosseting of home life, but that I must learn to adapt to the discipline and be less flighty. I said nothing, but I was secretly amused at her vision of home life, which did not resemble very closely my own experience. Matron said she thought I was still a bit young for the job and that I would spend the next three months in the baby nursery attached to the maternity ward, "Mary". Duly chastened, I went to the new ward which proved to be so peaceful it was all I could do to keep awake during the long hours of baby care.

We all worked very long hours, going on duty at 7 a.m., making beds, dusting and cleaning, and tidying the patients and their lockers. The flowers reposing in the sluice at night (so as not to breathe up all the oxygen) had to be tidied up and returned to the right patient. All this before morning prayers at 9.30 led by sister. Then we worked until 10.30 and had half an hour off to change our aprons and "coffee".

We did so many "menial" tasks, helping Sister out with the meals, serving drinks, emptying and cleaning sputum mugs, as well as the tasks nowadays thought to be within a nurse's proper duty such as dressings, blanket baths, enemas, taking out stitches, and administering drugs. The "Pinkies", marvellous ward maids, Lambeth characters to a woman, did the floor washing and polishing, but we were responsible for the "high dusting", tidiness in the kitchen when the Pinkie had washed up and most particularly supervising meals. Patients were allowed to bring in their own eggs and we would boil them for their tea. Bed pan rounds happened three or four times a day, and as so few patients got up this was a major job and we grew adept at carrying seven or eight down the ward from the sluice. Most patients needed help in heaving themselves on to them. Then there were "backs" to be done and often heels too. We took immense pride in preventing bed sores occurring, which was just as well because once formed healing was a slow if not impossible process.

In those days we were thought to be delicate and our health was quite carefully nurtured. The food was superb and for elevenses we had a choice of numerous dishes, left-overs, bread and butter, tomato soup and cakes and puddings of all sorts. Nurses who looked "off colour" were given a glass of stout at dinner and, when in the sick bay, a glass of sherry before meals.

As I became rather more confident I found the work quite engrossing. I was deeply impressed throughout my training by the immense courtesy we were taught to show to patients and relatives, the importance of which was instilled in us from the first days. We were told the patients and relatives were our guests and must be treated as such and it was our privilege to take care of them. No visitor was ever left hanging about outside the ward trying to catch someone's eye but was immediately approached by any passing nurse to find out what was needed. Telephone enquirers were dealt with equally courteously and referred to Sister quickly. We were taught to answer any patient's request with the utmost speed, however inconvenient it might be to us, and to be constantly aware of what was happening to the patients under our care and their state of mind.

In those days patients spent much longer in the wards so we really had time to get to know them. One of the reasons for this was because modern drugs such as penicillin were not yet on the market and patients with infections such as pneumonia or cardiac failure needed intense bedside nursing and there were no special care units. On the other hand I never saw an adverse drug reaction and allergies were virtually unheard of. Nor were there heroic measures to prolong life and the dying were able to die with grace and comfort. Morphia and heroin were prescribed liberally to cancer patients and although we all saw terrible suffering I can only recall one patient who died in fear and pain.

It is often said that nurses must, by the very nature of their work, become hardened as they have to repress so much emotion and because of the constant exposure to suffering and death. There is obviously some truth in this but I think we may have been protected by the way intense experiences were diluted by the constant preoccupation of routine and mundane tasks which brought us into contact with the patients but did not constantly expose us to their suffering. We had so many routines to think of we had barely time to feel in any case. When we made the beds, for instance, all the pillow case openings had to face away from the door, castors on the beds had to be dusted and turned in and each counterpane immaculately "enveloped". So although it could be argued that we learnt to respond to pain and take care of dying patients and to lay out the dead as another routine, I think this is only partially true and that we just coped with suffering at our own pace. Then too our psychic energy was spread over a wide field: there were the numerous lectures to attend, we had to prepare for exams, and for Sister's supervision of a newly-learnt technique. Nearly all our off duty time was spent in studying and keeping our notes up to date. I remember thinking about and caring for the patients with great concern and tenderness but a lot of energy also went into a desire to achieve, to keep up, to do things properly and not to be found out if I did not.

The quality of the lectures we attended was superb, even though one was often too exhausted to attend properly and it was hard to keep awake, particularly after night duty. But I loved the lectures and soaked it all up like a thirsty animal at an African watering hole. We were taught by eminent consultants who presented the material so well I still remember much of what we learnt particularly about medical conditions. I was less enthusiastic about surgery but an interest in medicine has stayed with me all my life. In the same way I preferred physiology to anatomy, the latter seemed to me to be too static to be interesting. We had to learn about the flow of blood and the complicated functions of the liver and the kidneys. It was all sheer delight to me and murmuring "the heart is not easily fatigued" I would carefully crayon one more diagram of the heart with its mysterious and wonderful valves and chambers. Lectures were followed by tutorials from the sister tutors and occasionally theory and practice came together on the wards when Sister had time to teach us, but there were no clinical instructors and it was all rather hit and miss, I suppose. You might be learning about the three stages of typhoid infection but be in a surgical ward dealing with the usual run of Metropolitan policemen and their perforated gastric ulcers.

St. Thomas' was the hospital used by the Metropolitan Police, and many came in with ulcers and pneumonia; the latter contracted, one suspects, by drinking alcohol before going out into a bitterly cold night under the illusion that the drink would keep them warm. The police were very helpful in the ward, volunteering with the tea round and other chores as soon as they were up and about. Nowadays as an activist with C.N.D. and the Animal Rights Movement, I'm constantly in touch with the police in a different set of circumstances, but as I often tell them having seen so many naked policemen in my youth quite diminishes any intimidation I might otherwise feel. It was a member of the C.I.D. in the ward recovering from an operation for a double hernia who kindly lent me his copy of "Lady Chatterley's Lover", not at that time obtainable legally. I was most grateful to him and longed for the day I might weave daisy chains to decorate my loved one's penis, though I am sure the actual word never reached my conscious mind.

Nightingale nurses were not exposed more than necessary to anything indelicate or as potentially shocking as the male genitalia. In the preliminary training school we were taught about male and female anatomy behind drawn curtains with the lecture room doors firmly closed. Male ward orderlies shaved male patients with an open cut throat razor when this was necessary below the waistline, and if a man needed catheterising this too was done either by a male student or doctor. Blanket baths were done with due respect for modesty, usually two nurses working together behind the screen. Having bathed the whole patient except for his or her private parts, we would hand him or her a soaped flannel saying "I expect you would like to finish off," and leave for a minute closing the screens carefully behind us. No one ever questioned what we meant. We gave enemas, of course, and rubbed buttocks to prevent bed sores so we must have had an occasional glimpse of testicles. I took all this for granted. I was still somewhat sexually unawakened and incurious and remained so until my mid-twenties. Men were people and I liked them but I had no erotic feelings towards them and never met any socially. I continued to take little interest in my appearance off duty and wore no make-up, although when on duty I took pride in my immaculate uniform and brushed my hair back severely, so that as a friend said, "You look like an egg with a frill on it".

Relationships with medical students and doctors were not encouraged, though we were advised in the preliminary training school that it was quite in order to exchange courtesies should one be washing hands at the ward basin at the same time. There was an archetypal story of a nurse being instantly dismissed for kissing a student in the linen cupboard. Whether this was because of the nature of the transaction, or because this might have disarrayed that sacred cupboard with all the sheets and pillowcases facing the same way, is unknown. We were also told that if we should begin an alliance with a medical student we should not meet our friend under Big Ben as this was very conspicuous. We were not allowed to marry during training. In spite of these restrictions or perhaps because of them St. Thomas' nurses did marry doctors quite frequently. I was definitely retarded and simply thought of the medical students as superior beings (though not as superior as Sister) and the doctors who wrote out the prescriptions and were instantly available in an emergency were not individuals to me. Although sometimes I thought an individual houseman or registrar looked delectable, I did not fall in love, weave romantic dreams, let alone daisy chains for him, in fact or in fantasy.

CHAPTER TWELVE

LIZ

1938 - 1943

One of the joys of nursing training was that of conviviality - the esprit de corps, the friendships that came of being in a set. These were particularly intense in the first two years before we scattered to war hospitals out of London, leaving only a nucleus of trained nurses to cope with London casualties. There was dear Jean, a mature young woman quite some years older than the rest, who acted in her proper role of mother by being "at home" for tea and biscuits and general comfort. There was Lucy whom we instantly recognised as a "True Nightingale" (T.N.) who would of course in time become a matron, as indeed she did; and poor Pip who seemed to have chronic heart failure from the day she came, although she stood the course for a year. There were other friends: kind Trudy with her long flaxen hair who would always wake me up in the morning and Penny who became a boon companion second only to Liz, who became my closest and dearest friend for the next four years.

I got to know Liz in the first year when she introduced me to the world of music, politics and literature, and lent me books to read. Soon we were exchanging notes every day and contrived to spend as much time as we could off duty together. Ours was never an overt lesbian relationship, more in the nature of David and Jonathan (surely there must be a feminine equivalent?). Liz was never well, constantly chain smoking and lived, as she said, as if "Time's wingèd chariot" was always behind her, as it sadly proved to be. She was thin and lived with an intensity far removed from my fundamentally quiet orientation to the world. I could see that we complimented each other. Her pet name for me was either Modestine, the burden-bearing donkey in Stevenson's book, or Seal, no doubt because I seemed a placid smooth character with eyes gazing out in some wonderment and interest on the world. For me she was life itself.

Liz thought herself neurotic, self-preoccupied and moody, but there was reciprocity in our mutual dependence. I comforted her and searched for the delicacies she liked and did my best to shelter her, and she gave me the world in exchange. Soon we were going together to the National Gallery concerts which began soon after war broke out. They were held in the lunch hour and cost a shilling entrance with a penny for the programme. We heard Myra Hess on numerous occasions and Dennis Matthews playing Beethoven sonatas, Harry Isaacs playing César Franck's Choral Prelude and Fugue and Robert Irwin singing, "Now Sleeps the Crimson Petal" and Arne's "Come Away Death". From Matron's office nurses could get theatre, ballet and concert tickets almost on demand, provided one could rustle up an evening dress. Liz and I went to Sadler's Wells Ballet rehearsals and to the Albert Hall for the Proms. She taught me about art and shared with me her own love for Blake, and for the poets Herbert, Marvell and Donne. We tried whenever possible to get our days off together so that we could go to her home in Appleford in Berkshire where more delights of music awaited me. I lay in a trance listening for the first time to Chopin and to the Messiah and to the Bach mass and Beethoven concertos. I cannot imagine that I was at all discriminating, I just let it all flood over me. As in the convent, it was another renaissance. We shared our love for her black sleek cat, Virgin. During those years animals took a less prominent place in my life than they would later on, but I thought Virgin adorable and loved watching the animals in the Berkshire countryside. Rabbits in fields of buttercups and the squirrels in the chestnut trees.

Our set was the last to live in the old Nightingale home, Gassiot House, bombed during the war and now replaced by a modern nurses' home overlooking Westminster Bridge. We were cosseted in our first year in a way which would seem quite extraordinary to a modern nurse. We were not allowed to go on night duty as this was felt to be a health hazard, but at the end of the first year, should we survive the killing pace, we were given a month's holiday and then went on night duty for three months as staff nurses, perhaps so that we should be fairly invisible while we were taking on our new responsibilities. A change in status was marked by being ejected from Home Sister's watchful and caring eye, and we missed her. We were really now in the deep end, no longer probationers, no more cleaning, but considered to be responsible for patients' care, usually as a "second" to a trained nurse in a ward of thirty or more patients. Wearing our new uniforms and very conscious of our status we took immense responsibility, administering drugs and caring for the acutely ill through the long night. We worked from 8 p.m. to 7 a.m. and then went to supper. This was usually followed by a lecture and it was hoped that we could get out for some fresh air after this. We were not permitted to wear our uniform off duty at all for fear of contamination, except to walk in Lambeth Palace Gardens, to which we had the key. This lovely place became one of my sanctuaries and huddled in the warm navy and scarlet cloak I would sit with a book watching the birds or stroll with Liz if by a lucky chance she was off duty too.

Soon after our first spell of night duty war was declared. I had not really appreciated what was happening in the world. I still never read a newspaper but I was sufficiently aware of pending events to discuss my pacifist views with anyone who would listen. As there were so many nurses with fathers in the armed forces, my audience was limited, except of course Liz, who shared my views. But on one occasion when I was expounding Gandhian and Albert Schweitzer philosophy in the ward kitchen a nurse said to me "with your views you should join the Quakers." This was one of those significant remarks that once again changed my life. The same girl told me how to find Friends House, and I began attending Quaker meetings for worship with Liz and quite soon we applied for membership. I was drawn to Friends because of their peace testimony and because they seemed to me to try and live out their religion in daily life, particularly in social reform. I liked the saying of William Penn, "Walk cheerfully over the world seeking that of God in every man," which reminded me no doubt of Kim and his philosophy of being a friend to all the world. I was also fascinated by the life of John Woolman, that great reformer with his courage to be "peculiar". I was a bit overawed by it all from the beginning and I sometimes thought that Friends were too good, too conventional and too middle class. I stayed in the Society for many years until in time I began to feel that it was paternalistic and gave too little credence to the power of evil. I became conscious that the Christian church was a church for sinners and the Quakers seemed to me to be short of conscious sin. But during the war and for many years after that Friends played a significant role in my spiritual life and in supporting me in my radical views in relation to non-violence.

After war broke out, the Nightingale nurses, as many as could be spared, were sent out to war hospitals scattered around southern England taking over mental hospitals, asylums (as they were then called), or institutions for the mentally handicapped. We went first to Park Prewett Hospital, Basingstoke, where we had a boring few months with only a few patients to nurse, then to Botley's Park, Chertsey, which quickly filled with casualties from the forces and civilian life, mostly suffering from medical conditions, not war wounds. The wards were in separate blocks known as Huts, and we lived in cubicles in one of these and ate in another. It was a far cry from the comparative luxury and cloistered atmosphere of our mother hospital. We were put in charge of forty- to forty-five bedded wards often with only V.A.D.s to assist us. On looking at a list of the forty-five male patients in Hut 4, dated January 27th 1941 where I was the third nurse in charge on night duty, I see there were four men there with advanced lung tuberculosis, eight with cardiac failure, five with lobal pneumonia, two with ulcerative colitis, ten with gastric ulcers or colitis, three with cardiac complications and the rest with kidney failure, influenza and anthrax. There was still no penicillin but we were now using the first of the sulphonamide drugs. Tuberculosis was still rampant and did not wane in this country until people were better nourished and housed. It then declined rapidly prior to the discovery of the specific drugs to treat it. Perhaps infections were also more easily resisted because of rationing enabling poor people to obtain better quality food and free milk.

At the beginning of our third year of training I became really concerned about Liz's health. She was so thin and exhausted and her sad though funny notes complaining of perpetual fatigue kept us in constant communication even when we were on different shifts and wards. She wrote to me, "But remember that there is music and civilised pursuits in Herbert and Donne and cats and bookshops and sun and sea and holidays somewhere behind it all, not only beds and medicines and dressings, do believe that." She could not sleep when we were on nights and helped herself liberally to medications available on the ward and I would add to her store with handfuls of barbiturates without much concern for the moral question. Many nurses took sedatives in order to sleep and I remember being slightly shocked at seeing one of my pals lean out of bed and take a swig from a bottle of bromide mixture she had hidden behind her locker. This was not my problem and although I was tired like everyone else I felt fit and well and even the disturbed nights with incendiary bombs falling in the grounds did not unduly disturb my equilibrium. I did not really follow the course of the war very closely, being too pre-occupied with worry about Liz and our training, but I continued to dream about India, and I determined to go and work in Bengal when I was qualified to help combat disease and misery. Meanwhile, I heard that my brother Peter who had been working as an engineer on a tea plantation, had later joined the army and had been captured at Singapore and taken to a Japanese prisoner of war camp.

In Chertsey, I watched sadly as Liz got thinner. I thought she had cancer or tuberculosis. From time to time she was summoned for a medical check but no organic cause was found for her loss of weight. She did not seem to eat much, but was adept at convincing me that she did. Penny, our friend, pointed out that she looked too ill to have any organic illness, as if she had it would be apparent by now. She thought that we should consider the possibility that there might be some nervous cause, but I did not know much about anorexia nervosa then. Life went on and towards the end of 1941 Liz was transferred to Hydestyle, near Godalming, where St. Thomas' was keeping the flag flying and the training by our own Sisters continued much as it did in the mother hospital. It was a few months before I followed Liz there. She was a patient there for a while, but she was back on the wards by the time I arrived. We had very comfortable lodgings together in the house up the hill where we were cosseted by the lady of the house.

After a time it became apparent to the authorities that Liz could not go on nursing. She was less than six stone in weight and although she gained a few pounds when she was a patient, she quickly lost this and more when she returned to duty. Liz was diagnosed as suffering from anorexia. We had very little psychological understanding and poor Liz was shattered when the nature of her illness was explained to her. In her eyes it was the most terrible disgrace to be ill with a psychological complaint, and she saw it only as a weakness and total failure to follow her chosen vocation. Yet it was, in a sense, some relief to her as she could not cope with the work and was perpetually exhausted. It was suggested that she should return to her home and rest for a few months to see how things went, but we both knew, as did the authorities, that this was the end of her nursing career.

From her home in Appleford Liz wrote daily about the frustrations and misery of not being able to work though she struggled bravely to be a good daughter to her invalid mother, who had taken to her bed some years previously with an unspecified complaint and never rose from it again. Liz shopped and cooked and was hospitable to visitors, practised the piano, talked to Virgin and wrote endless letters to me about how she had gained a pound in weight and all the food she had eaten that day. I did not really believe her, but she deceived herself, and she was not referred for any psychological counselling.

Meanwhile my mother had returned from South Africa and had set up house in Burnham Beeches. I visited her when I could and always dreaded these visits as I felt I never gave her enough time or loving care, but we went for walks together and I sometimes met her in London for shopping. She looked ill but never wanted to discuss her health. As she was terrified by hospitals I had the sense not to push this though I thought she probably had heart disease. She seemed happy enough with her spiritualist groups and a relay of feral cats who queued up at the back door for their rations. She was kind to all animals however unprepossessing and I remember her cutting up a piece of whale meat, which we had in those days, and flinging it to the waiting stray cats, then without washing her hands she put her arms around me to greet me or to say goodbye. She would also go out after dark to feed her hedgehog with a saucer of bread and milk. By the pale starlight he looked a bristly, shapeless object, not easy to tell which end of him was which. When he wanted to go down the rockery steps he folded himself in a ball and rolled down. In winter he hibernated in the rubbish heap.

Most of my off duty was spent in Appleford or in London with Liz. We had acquired, through a friend who had evacuated to the country, a little flat in Coronation Buildings in Lambeth Bridge Road and we used this as a base. Liz would try and get away most weekends and I would join her at the flat whenever possible, but it was getting near the time of my Finals and, as always, I put work first. Not even my concern for Liz would stop me revising. I have always found work a great stabiliser and have an absolute commitment to it which has always taken priority over relationships. Interesting and demanding work does offer a fine balance to turbulent emotions and I also knew instinctively that most of the things I wanted from life would come from work, and I still wanted the world. Many adults who have been deprived in childhood are very greedy, I think, and some survivors of abuse have a tenacity and will to live and achieve which may bring great rewards, although this may be accompanied by a streak of ruthlessness to self and others, as in myself.

Liz wrote encouragingly, though she thought my anxiety in regard to Finals quite unnecessary. But I continued to revise with my usual obsessional intensity, and soon Finals were over and I was a State Registered Nurse. In those days one stayed on an extra year following Finals and sat an internal examination to pass as a Nightingale Nurse and this was far more valued than the State Registration. This took place at the end of the fourth year so for some time I had a breathing space from exam anxiety and met Liz frequently. We slept together in our little flat, made toast in front of the coal fire, drank cider and talked endlessly. We went to concerts and art galleries and read T.S. Eliot and were not much concerned when the air raid warnings went off.

My final days at St. Thomas' were drawing near and I was back in the main hospital for a time, writing applications to midwifery schools because I wanted to go straight on to midwifery training. I knew that without this qualification I would not be of use in India and I also suspect that I unconsciously wanted to put away qualifications rather like a squirrel - my hidden capital for later, the equivalent of saving up for a rainy day.

Most hospitals in those days charged for midwifery training so I could not go to the hospital of my choice. After qualifying as a Nightingale Nurse I accepted instead a vacancy in Willesden which by good fortune had one of the finest obstetricians of the day lecturing to the students. The training was in two parts and I started the first six-month block in January 1943. We were so well taught that over forty years later when I went for a midwifery refresher course the theoretical knowledge was still quite fresh in my mind, which is more than I can say for any of the other academic courses I have taken.

I enjoyed the work and did not question the rightness of any of the procedures; women in labour had no say about how they would like their labour conducted and so flat on their backs they lay, poor things, or with their feet up in stirrups. Then when the baby was born it was quickly whipped away into the nursery to be produced for mother to see when she was rested and then fed regularly by the clock regardless of what she or the baby felt about it. Babies were clamped to the nipple by the firm and unrelenting grip of the attendant midwife and kept there for the allotted time. Small wonder then on the third day all the mothers were in tears and had engorged breasts, weeping over their babies or the breast pump. Husbands were not allowed to touch the babies and gazed at them through the glass windows of the nursery. In spite of all this some mothers did manage to breast feed and be happy but in those days we were all in the grip of the teaching of the New Zealand paediatrician, Truby King, and routine was all, but at least the babies were born without much obstetric interference.

I did not have any trouble coping with the syllabus and liked giving support to women in labour and comfort to the post natal depressed mothers. I was still far less confident at the practical side but I think I got away with it, to some extent, because of my air of confidence. But I remember one evening on night duty when I absent-mindedly made the evening cocoa with a jug of expressed breast milk by mistake - quick-witted as ever I explained the lack of expressed milk in the morning by saying I had dropped the jug, and of course experienced delinquent that I was, I covered up my tracks by actually breaking the jug for good measure. I was always terrified of being found out and one of the great joys and revelations in my later career was hearing psychiatrists, and even social workers, admit to their having made grave errors of judgement or having got it all wrong. But it was many years before I understood that it was all right to make mistakes both in acts and in judgement. The terrified child remained alive in me through most of my adult life, and still sometimes cries out when storm clouds gather, all ready with massive defences however out of proportion these may be.

During these months it was easy to see Liz every week and spend a night or two with her as by now nurses and midwives had far more time off duty. She was restless and unhappy at Appleford and wanted desperately to return to London and do some nursing. I thought of the Ranyard Nurses and on impulse, knowing their Christian commitment, telephoned the sister-in-charge and explained Liz's predicament. Her instant response, which I shall never forget was, "But of course we must help her and I am sure we can find her some home nursing which is within her strength." The sister-in-charge wrote to Liz saying, "Keep up your courage, remember that you are in the care of an all loving father and I know you will be of great use to us." Liz was interviewed and treated with the utmost Christian kindness and from then on given a small caseload to visit.

But one day when we met at the flat she seemed very ill indeed, sluggish and strange, and the next day she was almost comatose. I rang her mother and then took her to Lambeth Hospital where she was seen by the same physician who had seen her previously at St. Thomas' Hospital. That evening at a ward round when I was sitting by her bed he explained to the medical students that here was a clear case of conversion hysteria brought on by the stress of returning to nursing which had precipitated the anorexia nervosa in the first place. He demonstrated abnormal abdominal neurological reflexes as evidence. I felt guilty and angry with both Liz, the consultant and myself. When she was discharged the same day I was quite cross with her and she said, poor girl, "It may be all psychological but I don't feel well". I was relatively unsympathetic. Had I not been found to be in the wrong by encouraging her to do some nursing and been publicly shamed in front of the students by the consultant?

So Liz struggled back to work and I remember one day seeing her walking very unsteadily towards the bus stop. "She looks quite drunk," I thought, but she was not. The weeks went by and we spent weekends at Appleford during that lovely early spring and Liz seemed much the same. She complained that she could not play the piano as well as she used, and I made some facile reassuring remark, but she looked preoccupied as she tried to make her hands follow the keyboard.

Then one weekend at the London flat in May 1943 I saw her trying to light her cigarette with a match at least an inch away from the cigarette, and that same morning she laughed and said she saw two saucers and did not know on which one to place her cup. With terrible foreboding I asked the local general practitioner to visit and he confirmed what I had already guessed: that Liz had advanced multiple sclerosis. He said that it was a particularly virulent type and this accounted for the recent flare-up leading to the admission to Lambeth Hospital. Liz said, "In a way it's a relief to have something physical," then added, "but my attitude is typical of patients with this disorder" and she knew that euphoria was simply a symptom and that the condition was progressive and incurable. I had some leave due so we went to Appleford for a few days, but then Liz wanted to be in the flat so that she could be independent and we could meet more frequently. I rang up the consultant at Lambeth Hospital to tell him about what had happened and I hope he was duly shocked and would never again think that a history of neurosis precluded a physical disease.

I realise now that I was far too immature to be of much help to Liz in her last days. I loved her and took care of her but the situation was really beyond me. I had not suffered enough myself in adult life to be able to give her the support and understanding she needed. Although we were so close I did not know that she had assessed the future with clear eyes and decided it held nothing for her. "Time's wingèd chariot" had caught up with her faster than either of us had ever envisaged. On my day off on May 20th 1943 she greeted me lovingly and asked me to stop fussing around and to give her some attention. "Dear Seal," she said, giving me a hug, but her speech was very slurred and she seemed far away and quite suddenly she lapsed into unconsciousness. I ran out of the flat panic-stricken and telephoned one of her relatives, a cousin in London, who told me to order a Red Cross ambulance. When the cousin arrived we both knew Liz was dying and wanted to get her back to her own home. She was unconscious in the ambulance. Before leaving I looked around the kitchen for her toothbrush and saw without really comprehending a large empty bottle labelled, I believe, Bromide and Chloral, a sedative used in those days. The journey from London was desolate. Liz was alive but unconscious, breathing heavily and her red dressing gown was gradually stained with urine as she lost control of her bladder. I helped to carry her to her bed in Appleford. We sent for the general practitioner who knew her well. He said little but he gave her a morphia injection and left me another to give her should she be uncomfortable during the night, but she hardly stirred during the long night and just at dawn when I drew back the curtains, she died.

I stayed with her for a time, laid out her body and gathered some spring flowers to leave with her. Then I left for London and returned to the hospital. I was in a state of shock but my most overwhelming feeling as I sat on the underground train to Colindale was the most intense desire for a cigarette. I was a complete non-smoker and although Liz chain-smoked I had never been tempted to try a cigarette. If I had had a packet at the time I would have smoked one for her, but the feeling passed and did not return.

It was the end of an era: I would never have or expect to have such a friendship again, rich though my life has been in loving relationships, friendships and erotic encounters, but Liz, Liz, friend of my youth and my true soul mate left me so bereft that for years I felt like a hermit in the wilderness.

CHAPTER THIRTEEN

A MIDWIFE

1943 - 1945

Back at the hospital I had completed Part One of the training, had witnessed the required number of deliveries, conducted ten myself and sat the examination. I cannot remember much of that period as it was so clouded with grief for Liz. It was not my first or last exercise in such self control in the face of bereavement. Although I am never irritated by genuine grief in others, I think that I disliked shows of emotion and distrusted any show of feeling, at least in myself, perhaps because I had been so irritated by mother's pathos and maudlin behaviour. I grew, I think, to be arrogant, over-controlled and harsh to myself but I loved to see deep emotions expressed in art, particularly in opera and theatre, and still do. It is as if feelings are just fine provided they are stylised. On the other hand, in my professional life I have always been able to respond warmly and with real empathy to the raw emotions I meet in the course of work. I have no doubt that my extreme self control and calm has its darker side and many other feelings must still be buried with the griefs, holding back much potential creative energy.

Returning to hospital, I went on to the second part of the course, to practise home deliveries. This was spent in two centres; one in Burnt Oak and the other in Kensal Rise in London. Two midwifery pupils were attached to a qualified midwife and essentially apprenticed to her. Wherever she went we went, until towards the end we were conducting our own deliveries with the teacher not too far away. It was still war time and the blackout made some of our night journeys hazardous. I well remember biking through the pitch black night with only the dimmest of lamps, careering out of the way of buses looming like dinosaurs suddenly out of the gloom. Often there were pea-soup fogs too and it was freezing cold. Near our destination we were usually welcomed by a chink of light from a front door or window and a relative watching out for us. One of the joys of being a midwife was that one was always welcome, a sharp contrast to the reactions I later encountered as a social worker, and our work was highly valued by the community. So with my hunger for love and approval constantly met being a midwife was most fulfilling quite apart from the satisfaction of the work itself.

Midwives, whose practice was regulated by the rules of the Central Midwives Board and by field supervisors, were essentially conservative in their work. Their practice completely lacked the atmosphere of high technology and drama now found in maternity hospitals -where in my view many of the complications of delivery are caused by the tension induced in mothers by the technology itself. No doubt infant lives are saved but at what cost. Midwifery, in those days, was still predominantly in the hands of women and not yet taken over by male obstetricians except for the abnormal cases which we tried with some success to foresee. The general practitioner was on call if we needed him and the local hospital provided a home emergency service. Tiny premature babies did not always survive, but on the other hand problems of attachment and bonding between parents and infants were unlikely to occur with home deliveries since they were never separated. I do not recall seeing a single case of "baby blues" on the district and suspect that this was, at least in part, because the mother was in control of her life in her own home. Then again we did not call out the doctor to sew up every tiny perineal tear, though we were supposed to, so many tears healed of their own accord and episiotomies, i.e. cutting the mother's tissue to deliver the baby, were rare. That procedure has been linked with post natal depression and the stitches make for great discomfort and the pain may lead to frigidity later. But this is no place to air my views on the horrors of modern obstetrics. The pendulum in any case is now beginning to swing back.

So the weeks went by and I became deeply absorbed in the work, enjoying the responsibility and contact with families in the home. I was amazed by the warmth and casual lifestyle of the Irish families, many of whom would do nothing to prepare for the confinement until the last possible moment. We would despair at the disorder in the home, wondering if the place would ever be put straight in time for the delivery, but it always was. All our careful instructions were adhered to down to the smallest detail, the baby clothes warming on the fire-guard, hot water bottle in the cot or drawer prepared with clean bedding for baby, the water on the boil, basins at the ready, the empty paste pot for the thermometer, the bed made up with rubber mackintosh and piles of newspaper on hand to protect the floor and for wrapping up dirty swabs and the placenta, which later would crackle merrily on the fire after we had carefully examined it in a bucket of water. Each crackle and pop was supposed to indicate a future pregnancy and many a groan would come from the mother as she noted these sitting up drinking her tea and watching us bath and dress her baby soon to be cradled in her arms and put to the breast. Sometimes during air raids we moved our patients to a safer place, away from windows, on the floor under the table.

Labour generally tended to be longer than it is now in hospital but the slower pace was less painful than it sometimes is with accelerated deliveries. If there was any cause for concern about progress we would send for an ambulance at once, not necessarily even waiting for the general practitioner to give an opinion. No doubt terrible disasters did occur, though I myself have never seen a mother die in labour. But I recall one terrifying case which seemed to have gone quite normally. There had been no haemorrhage or delay and I was peacefully bathing baby when the mother said, "Isn't it getting dark early?" As it was still broad daylight I was most alarmed and indeed the mother seemed to be slipping into deep shock. We were in hospital within half an hour. I had given such treatment as I could meanwhile and she lived. The cause remained a mystery and I can only think it was some sort of reaction to the drug routinely administered following the delivery of the afterbirth.

Following each birth we were required by law to stay at least an hour to make sure the womb was properly contracted and that there was no bleeding. We usually stayed longer and had tea with the family. In those days it was more often "Camp" coffee and the sight of a bottle of this on the supermarket shelves still gives me acute nostalgia and not only because of the Sahib and his bearer on the label! The midwife who was supervising the case would finish the last stitch of the baby socks she had been knitting and present them to the mother and we would wrap the dirty linen ready for the bag wash - no washing machines in those days - pack up our delivery bags, retrieve our bicycles from a hall or kitchen often with the tyres nicely blown up by a male relative and set off home exhausted and happy. Delivering babies under these conditions is not only a "high" for the family, including brothers and sisters, but for the midwives in attendance at the event.

At home we would sterilise, re-pack our bags, write up our cases and either sleep if we were off duty or go on duty if we were not. We would revisit our patient the same evening or first thing in the morning, then twice a day for three days, and then daily until the baby was a fortnight old. We allowed mothers to get up on the third day, but many would get on with household tasks in bed, shelling peas and peeling the potatoes. There were few women available to help mothers during the war as they were all in the factories or in the forces, but husbands were often given compassionate home leave for a period and so there was a great family reunion and babies got off to a good start. Although it was before the days when it became fashionable for fathers to stay with their wives in labour, with home deliveries the couple did as they liked and only a few midwives would exclude the husbands from the birth if this was desired.

Six months drew to a close with Finals looming and I was as usual studying rigorously. I had no difficulty with the theoretical papers - whether I would have done or not with the practical I will never know because my patient on whom I had to give a diagnosis and opinion hissed at me, bless her, "You can see the scar? I had a Caesarean last time, I'm thirty-eight weeks and the head is high above the brim in the right lateral and extended. There is albumin in my urine, and if you can hear my blood pressure I'd be surprised, it's so high." I smiled at her gratefully, wished her a safe delivery and passed my examinations.

Never one to let the grass grow under my feet, I was already champing to get off to India where famine was raging in Bengal but no midwives could leave the country even had it been possible to go. I was already in touch with the Quakers about the possibility of working with them in India, and they listened to my inarticulate concern with gentle attention, suggesting that I write it all down before making a formal application. It was obvious that I would not be able to get away before the end of the war, so with a friend I set up as district midwife in Chelsea under the auspices of the London County Council who gave us a house and furnished it with regulation furniture, bicycles, uniforms and equipment.

By now I was twenty-three, tall, strong and plain and guaranteed I'm sure to give confidence to any expectant mother, dressed in a neat blue dress and apron, navy coat and pork-pie hat and with the midwifery box strapped firmly to the bicycle carrier. Our district was near World's End, Chelsea, although we sometimes covered the posher end of Chelsea for another midwife. At that time World's End consisted of streets and streets of little houses, all multi-occupied, and the people were very poor.

Because of the raids we lived mostly in the basement of our house, which was just as well because when a bomb fell nearby into the river much of the back of the house fell into the bedrooms. I slept in a cupboard under the stairs, telephone near at hand with a torch, candle, books and Emma - a delicious, long-haired tabby Persian cat I had acquired from my first patient. Emma had remarkable hearing as have most cats and could hear the buzz bombs and the V2s before I did and would dash to the cupboard to safety, closely followed by me, before the warning went off.

We held our clinic in the house, doling out the useless iron pills now no longer routinely prescribed to reluctant mothers. One of my favourite ladies, Mrs. Bubb, later told me that she gave all the pills to the chickens who then produced lovely eggs. Mothers with their families who had evacuated to the country in the early days of the war became homesick and returned to London in shoals. As there was no room for them in hospital unless it was the first baby or likely to be complicated, we were very busy with our home deliveries. I loved biking out at night and seeing the swans asleep by the river and although the air raids made the conditions of our work hazardous I was, as ever, more preoccupied with my daily work than with world events.

I had made some Indian friends and continued to read avidly about the country, especially the novels of modern Indians which were so vivid I felt I could be quite at home in the poverty and grim conditions of an Indian city. I read and re-read "Passage to India" and still followed the fortunes of the Indian fight for independence avidly, my sympathies, of course, with the Congress Party. In order to further prepare myself for work in India I did an enthralling course in tropical medicine. It was then that I came across a publication which was to channel my thoughts and determination, called "Maternal Deaths in Calcutta," by Dr. Neale Edwards and Dr. Jean Orkney. I wish I had it now. It was an account of a small research project in central Calcutta into the causes of maternal deaths over a limited period. At the end it made specific recommendations about how these deaths could be reduced by simple hygiene, better nutrition and the control of endemic disease in the mother, in particular malaria which caused fatal cases to occur from anaemia as the malarial parasite destroys red blood cells. I determined to go to Calcutta and follow through the recommendations in the report.

The war was drawing to a close and in 1945 I re-applied to the Friends Service Council who had a unit in Calcutta jointly run with the American Friends Service Council. I was accepted for a two year period as a volunteer relief worker. The next few months were spent in getting the necessary kit and various inoculations, rushing about in a frenetic way. My poor friend, who had hoped to go on sharing the district work with me for some time, was thrown back on her own resources as I began to cast off.

Then there was Emma. I know there will be amongst the readers of this book people who are as devoted to animals as I am, and because of this I do not intend to write much about animal sorrows as it does not do any good and it only haunts one. But to show some aspect of my ruthlessness when pursuing my own ends, I must tell that I had darling Emma put to sleep because I did not trust anyone else with her. Curled up on my lap in the taxi on the way to the vet she seemed to know and lay trustingly until we reached the office and there died instantly under a barbiturate injection, voicing no protest. I now find my behaviour incomprehensible and I could not leave my animals for any inducement. But India was my destiny then. I felt impelled to go and nothing could be allowed to stand in my way. The seeds laid down in the little primary school in Pinner, those hours with Mowgli and Baloo paddling up the Ganges, the later intellectualisation of all this in my identification with the Gandhian cause and my desire to help Indian mothers and babies all added up to a longing to serve in India which I felt as a clear call that could not be denied. Indeed, there were no questions in my mind; sorrow about Emma and her premature murder, but otherwise no regrets.

CHAPTER FOURTEEN

INDIA AT LAST

1945

The Quakers obtained permission from the Government of India for me to join the Calcutta unit and booked a passage on the S.S. Strathnaver for a berth to Bombay costing £63, sailing from Southampton on the 14th October 1945. The passage notification came by letter from the Office of the High Commissioner of India with awful warnings that the ship would be fully berthed under wartime austerity arrangements, stressing that conditions would be "austere in the extreme, when judged by peace-time standards and may occasion a degree of discomfort which is inevitable and must be accepted." I did not foresee this personally causing me any problems and carefully stencilled my name on the black tin trunk without which, of course, no one ever travelled. Had I not seen similar black tin trunks stacked on Waterloo Station since I was a child in the days when missionaries and Memsahibs and colonial officials set out regularly to serve in India and darkest Africa so that the sight of a topee casually crowning the cabin luggage carried in my imagination all that I would one day experience myself? Now at last in my twenty-sixth year I was setting out for the kingdom of my imagination; my mind well stocked with Bengali poetry, Gandhian philosophy, E.M. Forster in my cabin luggage, a map of India in my heart and a longing to bring the benefits of the London County Council Midwifery Service to Calcutta mothers and babies.

If I had not been so thrilled to be travelling to India the journey would have been tedious as the boat served as a troop ship and there were only four other women aboard, all army nurses. No alcohol was allowed on board and this made the officers and men gloomy. I have never been skilled in casual social relationships and so made no friends and I should really have given my mind to learning Bengali. There were a couple of other Quaker volunteers aboard who were destined to join the Quaker China Convoy and they were engrossed in learning Chinese. It is a matter of great shame to me that I never learnt any foreign language properly and never in my service overseas have I got beyond the most elementary standard. If I had been American and joined the Peace Corps, language competence would have been compulsory and instruction laid on, but without this kind of discipline I was blocked by laziness and a serious lack of confidence in my linguistic ability. This has not stopped me travelling extensively all through my life and I am still dreaming of other, so far, unvisited far horizons.

Once again I was on a long sea voyage sailing towards the Southern Cross, the phosphorescence and flying fish. Our route lay around the Cape of Good Hope because the Suez Canal was still closed, so our journey took nearly three weeks. I dreamt the time away, intensely happy to be sailing into the Arabian Ocean at last, day after day bringing India nearer. I remembered my dreams of running away as a child, of finding a boat to take me away from home to India . I knew that Peter, recently liberated from the Japanese camp, was now in India working on a tea plantation in Assam and that he might meet me in Bombay.

In the days when one still went by sea to India, the first sight of the great subcontinent was the marble archway known as the Gateway to India, standing at the entrance of Bombay Harbour. Then we were at the docks and I eagerly scanned the crowds. Peter was instantly recognisable, and I felt a tide of emotion when I saw him looking terribly thin, standing a little apart from the teeming people. Once disembarked, he quickly had me through Customs and in a rickshaw, and told me that he had booked me into the posh Taj Hotel. I thought this was not at all what the Quakers would have wished but did not know how to deal with the situation. He had already been in touch with the Unit in Calcutta who had told him tactfully that Friends did not travel First Class in a train so he had compromised and booked Second Class. Later I learnt that Friends travelled everywhere Third Class or by bus on shorter distances, but Peter, naturally, had definite ideas about the status of Memsahibs. That evening he took me for a drink at the European Club and then saw me safely back to the luxurious hotel. By then it was dark and I quickly changed into a simpler dress and sandals and slipped out into the night. I wanted to see the city and to feel that I had landed. It was still, of course, the days of the Raj although these were drawing to a close, so it was natural that Peter would regard any deviance from the rules as unacceptable behaviour. I was sure that he would not think it right that I should walk around the streets at night alone.

Nowadays with television and the heightened awareness of poverty in Third World countries, the scenes which I saw that first night in India would be little cause for comment and indeed I was not surprised as I was aware from books of the terrible conditions. Nevertheless, the visual and emotional impact was extreme. I found myself in a narrow winding lane threading through the *bustees*, the homes of the homeless and dispossessed, made of mud and dung and occasionally of corrugated sheeting and cardboard. Sacking was strung from the door-frames to give some privacy and little fires with iron pots of rice gave off an acrid smoke, fanned by crouching women wrapped in threadbare cloth. Children played in the dust and the emaciated cows and the occasional goat wandered about picking at the rubbish heaps. The Indian smell compounded of incense, dung, spice and orange blossom hung in the air. I stopped for tea, served in a brass vessel, at a little stall and a young girl came out with her baby sister balanced on her hip. We smiled at each other as she fingered my dress and made me understand that my wrists devoid of bangles were strange. There was some discussion among the women and I understood that they assumed I was widowed. My dress was faded and would have passed for white - the colour of mourning - allowing for cultural variations of its pastel shade. I wore no rings and thus my marital status seemed assured. Another child came up and gave me a marigold and after a time holding this and making the Hindu gesture of farewell - palms of hands folded in front - I wandered back through the smoky shadows to the hotel. All around on the pavements and between the flowerbeds men were sleeping out in the open, their faces covered with a cloth against the night air and mosquitoes. I put a rupee into one frail unclasped hand knowing this was only a gesture but it seemed the only offering I could make that night.

Next day Peter saw me off on the Calcutta Express and I settled into the marvellous endless journey across the subcontinent, complete with bedding roll, sunglasses and baggage safely stowed under the seat. I was in a ladies compartment and shared the journey with a cultured Bengali mother and her children. The husband in the next compartment visited from time to time to make sure we were comfortable and wanted for nothing. Two days and two thousand miles later we streaked into Hoogley Station, where I was glad to be met by members of the Unit. I was driven to Upper Wood Street and some hours later, having showered off layers of dust, I was drinking tea with my new companions.

The house was simply furnished, with a pleasant garden, and was used as an office and for temporary hospitality for volunteers en route for the Quaker China Convoy and for anyone who happened to be in town or had newly arrived. Meetings were also held there and Sunday worship. Most of the twenty or so volunteers were on projects out of town, working in fishing co-operatives in Chittagong, on milk distribution programmes or in village community development. A number of Bengali volunteers were attached to the Unit and it was from these old hands that I began to learn something about the country. In 1945 there were only two more years to go before Indian independence. Bengal was still undivided and Pakistan and Bangladesh were not yet in existence. There was considerable communal unrest. The anti-British feeling was at its height and there was some mob violence, but in the last days of the Empire the old order continued amongst the British and the Friends Unit was a unique oasis of inter-cultural exchange and fellowship. Some members of the Unit felt it right to cultivate Indian politicians and tried to influence events from the top; others worked with Congress and communist volunteers to try and help relieve some of the grinding poverty in the villages. The Bengal famine was over, but it had left a trail of devastation in cities and villages.

Soon after I arrived there was a tidal wave which came in the wake of the monsoon, flooding hundreds of villages, and the Indian Red Cross appealed to Friends for volunteers to help them in the emergency. An epidemic of cholera had broken out in the stricken villages now marooned on mud banks without food or medical supplies. I was assigned to go with the Red Cross medical students team to help with inoculations and the distribution of food and to join a group led by Jamini Sarkar, a tea importer. As we had to spend so much time together living in a little boat Jamini said he would adopt me as his sister so that I would be under his fraternal protection. Later when we were back in Calcutta we consolidated this temporary arrangement with a Hindu festival, tying our wrists together so that we were bound in this fictive relationship for ever and we kept in touch for thirty years until he died.

We reached the stricken area by train and then hired boats. They were fishing boats with one end thatched over for shelter and sleeping. We took with us emergency army food rations and water purifying tablets as well as medical supplies, hurricane lamps and spades. The floods had begun to recede and little groups of villagers were marooned on the remaining patches of land. Not a tree nor a blade of rice remained, though many village homes were still standing. We split up into groups, each taking under our control several of the mud banks. We were, of course, all inoculated against cholera and in any case as long as we ate no contaminated food or water there was no danger to us from the disease. The health danger was from hookworm, which is conveyed through the skin from contaminated mud, but there was little we could do about that as we were tramping all day in the mud. The treatment of cholera, an acute intestinal infection, has changed since those days and at that time we knew less about rehydration - the replacement of fluids in the body. The infected villagers were lying in their rooms or out on the balconies with terrible "rice water" diarrhoea pouring from them as they lay dying on the floor straight into what remained of the roads and into the pond. Our first job was to disinfect the water in the ponds, known as tanks, which we did with potassium chloride. We then gave inoculations from dawn to dusk while the medical students tried to save the lives of those already afflicted, working through the night by the light of torches and kerosene lamps. We set up saline drip infusions but in the first wave of the infections the illness was so virulent that most people died.

At the end of one day I sat on the mud bank with a young mother who had no milk left in her shrivelled breasts for her tiny baby. I made up some powdered milk and she put this in a shell and finding a straw bent it so that one end was in the milk and the other lay against her nipple. Then she put the baby's mouth to her nipple and the infant sucked feebly and was able to draw up the powdered milk solution. I stayed with mother and baby all night to make sure all was well, and by morning the baby was sleeping contentedly. I fetched food supplies for the mother, whose name was Nilima and we were able to reunite her with her own parents who were marooned on an adjoining mud bank. Her husband and other children had died in the epidemic.

Each night when we were not working my Indian brother and I slept in our little boat. There was just room for two. In the morning he would dig me a fresh latrine and surround it with a roll of bamboo screen so that I could wash and use the lavatory in privacy. As I was the only woman in the team I very much appreciated this kind regard for my modesty and privacy.

Within two weeks the epidemic was under control and by then Government relief was arriving and we could withdraw and return to Calcutta. I was glad to get back to the Unit for a bath and a cooked meal, and felt satisfied that I was now truly in India and that my nursing training had been worthwhile. But I had not considered the side-effects of living in a fishing boat for weeks.

On the first evening back I went with a friend to hear E.M. Forster talking about English Literature to the Calcutta University. I sat at the back of the hall enthralled, but became conscious that my head, for some reason, felt very itchy! Back at the Unit I discovered that I had all three forms of lice on my person. My friends thought this hilarious and helped clean me up with liberal quantities of D.D.T. powder which they helped comb through my hair. I did not like to tell Jamini of this embarrassment as it seemed immodest to mention it.

My next assignment was to spend a month in Santineketan, "Abode of Peace", the home of Rabindranath Tagore, to nurse his daughter who was unwell and to begin lessons in Bengali. Santineketan was not at that time a university but there was considerable community work taking place in the villages round about: spinning and weaving for the women and other village crafts taught in the light of Gandhian philosophy.

I think I was too shy and gauche to feel totally at ease in this atmosphere although I was amazed to find myself in the Tagore country remembering my dreams of Tagore's poetry when I was in South Africa. It was a disadvantage in India to be tall and well built as I was, so this accounted for part of my embarrassment. I was always stiff jointed and not for me the lotus or even the semi-lotus position. It was as if my body image was out of tune with my love for and identification with the country. I felt clumsy and stupid at times, conscious too of the ancient culture and of my ignorance, but I felt spiritually at home and in time this overcame my sense of uneasiness.

I was taught Bengali by the direct method using as a basis the school books written for little children by Tagore. Page one began I remember: "In the forest dwelt the tiger, in the water dwelt the fish," and I managed to master the elements of Bengali script and indeed found this fascinating. At night I had my nursing duties and watched over my patient, admiring the huge fire flies lighting up on the mosquito net. During my time there, the Santal tribal people came to dance all night at the time of the full moon and I joined them swaying back and forth in semi-circular lines of linked bodies to the sound of drums. Everyone had drunk a great deal of todi, a delicious alcoholic drink made from the date palm, much disapproved of by missionaries.

Mahatma Gandhi was expected and one afternoon we gathered silently on the grass waiting for him. He was delayed, the sun went down and the feeling of expectancy increased. Villagers from far and wide had gathered to do him honour and the women of the household had been busy preparing for his simple meals. At last a great sigh of joy came from the crowds and shouts of "Mahatma Gandhi Ki jai" (Mahatma Gandhi comes) as a slight figure walked to the rostrum. Garlanded with orange blossoms he spoke to us about the need to work in the villages and the joys of living a life of Ahimsa (harmlessness). At the end of the meeting as I was standing quietly at the side, Dr. Sushila Nayar took me by the hand to meet Gandhi and he stopped for a minute as I was presented. A lamp was held up so that his face only was circled in light. I bent to touch his feet and felt profoundly moved and honoured. He was a man who radiated power, health, spiritual vigour and confidence.

I returned to Calcutta in December, the coolest time of the year, the monsoon having cleared the stagnant air and washed the trees and buildings so that for a brief period it was comfortable to live there. The little green parakeets flew in the suburban gardens and Mrs. Bumble, the Unit's white and ginger cat, presented us with three kittens which she carefully nursed in the filing cabinet.

Bustees in Calcutta

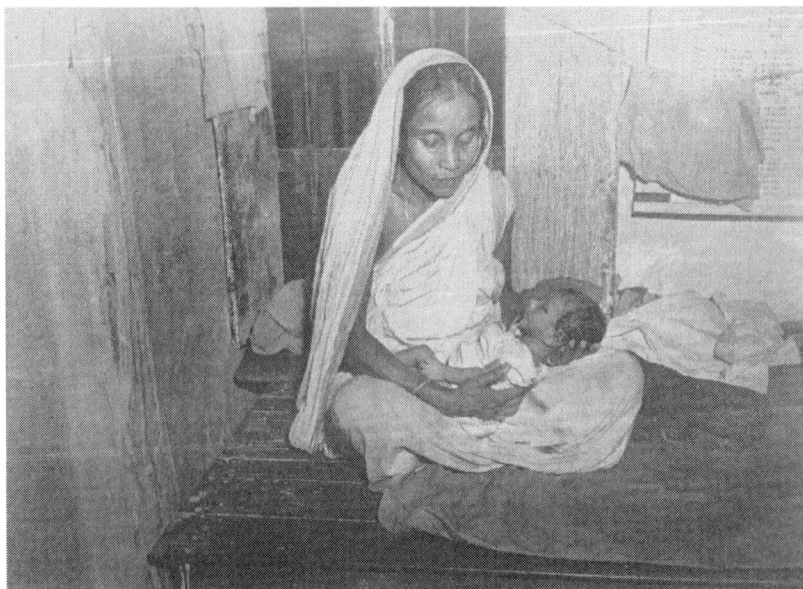

Rhada Rani with her baby

Discussing the new baby.
Five families to five rooms in one middle class Muslim home

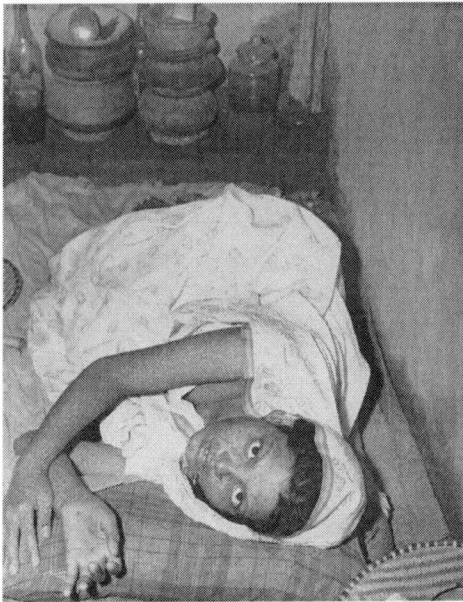

Recovering from smallpox

Mrs Raza demonstrates delivery techniques to indigenous midwives

Bela Bannerjee

Indian village children

East Bengali Village

Muslim homes Calcutta 1945/6

Bustees in Keshab Sen Street near where I worked

Bela receiving her S.R.N. Certificate from Lady Mountbatten

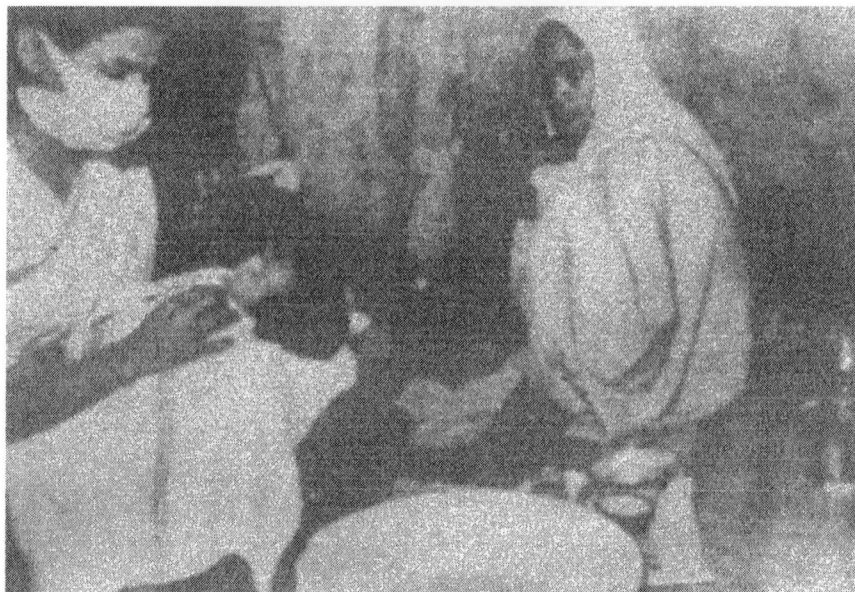

Nihar with Rhada Rani - showing her how to bath her baby

GANDHI 1946

CHAPTER FIFTEEN

CALCUTTA MOTHERS

1945 - 1946

It was time to get down to the project I had dreamed about as I biked around Chelsea's World's End. I was already growing quite apprehensive about this as one does when expected to bring dreams into reality. Fortunately Dr. Jean Orkney, the co-author of the research paper which had so influenced me, was still in the Colonial Medical Service in Bengal, and when we met she welcomed the idea of me attempting to implement her recommendations. She suggested that I live in the Maternity and Child Welfare Centre at the Sir John Anderson Health School in the centre of the city, where the research had been conducted, and work with staff and students there on a midwifery project. I expressed enthusiasm but felt quite reluctant to leave the relative comfort and security of the Quaker centre. But in mid-December 1945 I packed my things, assembled the midwifery kit and moved into my new home at 72,Sitaram Ghosh Street with my new colleagues, the three Hindu girls who ran the Centre. The area was a mass of little winding streets in a Hindu area with Kali temples scattered around as thick as pubs in an English city. The streets were unpaved and rubbish overflowed the open bins, thus supplying subsistence to the animal population: rats, wandering cows, buffaloes, cats, kittens and dogs. Some of the homes had running water but most of the population used the street pumps. The nearby houses were "pukka", made of stone and cement, and housed thousands of families of what one would call middle class, clerks, solicitors and students.

On the fringe of the immediate environment to the clinic were the homes of the very poor, – *bustees* – the shacks of the pavement dwellers. Many of these were immigrants from the villages, refugees from the famine area. Others had drifted into the city in the hope of making a living. Since partition these pavement dwellers have increased beyond measure and now constitute over a tenth of the population of Calcutta. Separated from our area by a paved road – Keshab Sen Street – which linked up with College Road, were other *bustees* which were to be the main target area of my project. It included a large Muslim area called Mechua Bazaar and a fruit market.

The health workers and the students gave ante-natal care and ran infant welfare clinics, but the actual deliveries were performed by the local *dais*, the indigenous midwives, and occasionally by the corporation midwives, though I never met any of the latter. Neither medical students nor hospital-trained midwives ever went out to the homes, let alone to deliver babies in them, and public health control was virtually non-existent. Every year smallpox raged through the centre of the city, babies born in the morning were often dead from tetanus by nightfall and the ravages of chronic amoebic dysentery, intestinal parasites and malaria left mothers and babies in particular in a state of chronic anaemia. The women were more vulnerable because of childbirth and the children because of their limited resistance. Then in all but the richer homes malnutrition was endemic. Many suffered from beriberi, a vitamin deficiency disease found among people whose main source of food is white polished rice. Leprosy was common, particularly amongst villagers coming into the city, and the scourge of poverty, lung tuberculosis, afflicted many of our patients who would casually interrupt their conversation to spit blood-stained sputum.

These were the days before the work of Mother Theresa had awakened the conscience of the nation and particularly that of the City fathers in Calcutta. Now, although the population of Calcutta has increased enormously and a terrible miasma of air pollution enshrouds the city, you seldom see anyone dying on the pavements or starving infants poking amongst the rubbish heaps. Mother Theresa with her saintly community and her work amongst the "poorest of the poor", did as much to bring relief to the suffering as the eradication of smallpox and the control of tetanus. But none of this had happened in 1945 and Calcutta resembled, I suppose, early nineteenth century Europe plus the mediaeval horrors of epidemic disease.

I wrote my first impressions in reports to the Quakers in England and America and immediately great stocks of medicines and vitamin supplements were despatched by Friends. We already had milk powder, which we made up each morning for distribution to the families.

By now I had an English speaking Bengali nurse, Bela Bannerjee, working with me. She had experience of working in *bustee* social service agencies and became one of my dearest life-long friends. Together we systematically visited all the families in the area, explaining that we wanted to help every pregnant woman as soon as she knew she was expecting the baby. The idea of early ante-natal care was new to people, but many families had seen a girl die in pregnancy and childbirth and we explained to the older women and to the men who controlled the families how we might be able to help. We contacted the local indigenous midwives, some of whom were already attending the centre for instruction, and we discussed with them how we might work together. We explained that after a few months we would not give care to any girl who did not register with our clinic before the fifth month of pregnancy, except in exceptional circumstances. We explained about the ravages of anaemia and that if this was not treated early in pregnancy it could lead to the mother's death. With a total disregard for caste customs we urged that the pregnant women should be given the cleanest area of the house for delivery, and we insisted on the most scrupulous hygiene possible in the circumstances. I am now rather ashamed of my ruthless attitude. I was not entirely unaware of taboos and customs but this awareness took second place in my determination to save the lives of mothers and babies regardless. Fortunately Bela was there at the time to filter and modify my more extreme expectations of our families and by the time she left for England some months later some of my desperate intensity was modified by circumstances and experience.

In the *bustees* we could not impose such rigorous demands. There were often at least eight people living in one room and our main fear was of tetanus because of the dried cow dung used for fuel. This was made into little round pancakes, plastered all over the wall by hand and pulled off when needed. The new-born babies who died from tetanus did so because of the dung-infected dressing put on the umbilicus by the *dais* or because a tetanus infected knife was used to cut the cord. Prevention was quite easy and no mother or baby died from tetanus amongst our deliveries. Our second great fear was of infection of the mother during delivery, or of haemorrhage from anaemia, but with intensive care during pregnancy anaemia could be alleviated and infections were averted by very simple hygienic control.

Bela and I were soon very busy and well accepted in the locality, particularly amongst the poor families. Although I knew in my heart that all our efforts were palliative, I remained fairly uninterested in the wider social and political issues. I recognised, I suppose, that most of the problems were insoluble unless there was a social revolution, but in the meantime all that I could do was to help relieve immediate suffering and hope that our project might demonstrate how much could be done with simple measures. I would get furiously angry on the rare occasions I met Europeans, other than members of the Unit, who would make comments such as: "What is the use of saving the lives of babies; it's only another mouth to feed?" Once I retaliated very rudely asking why a European baby's right to live should be thought more important than a child of a Bengali mother. I was accused of being an individualist or of "going native".

Once I was invited to talk to Lady Mountbatten whose great interest in nursing services was well known. It was pouring with rain and I set out from Sitaram Ghosh Street to Government House in a horse carriage, but the roof leaked and by the time I reached Government House I was dripping wet with hair plastered down my face. Even in a monsoon one could not wear protective clothing as it was still very hot, humid and sticky, and the most one could do for protection was to carry an umbrella. Still dripping, I was quickly made to feel that appearances did not matter as Lady Mountbatten asked penetrating questions about the condition of mothers and children in the city. She made me feel that our work was not only worthwhile, but that our own endeavours and those of our Indian colleagues were eminently sensible and appropriate.

I suppose the truly dedicated reformer and pioneer is less in need of encouragement from the establishment than I was but I have always sought and been glad of approval from the "respectables" as I have gone about my work. I do not think this comes from uncertainty about the rightness of the cause, whatever that may be, but from some basic fault in my psyche – a somewhat worm-eaten stratum of confidence that from time to time collapses under the weight of social disapproval. This has lessened over time and now I take some pride in being thought subversive or original. I remain, though, a faint hearted revolutionist, always wanting to be sound and orthodox while at the same time trying to push forward to some social revolution before it is generally accepted.

Life was not all work in Sitaram Ghosh Street. In the evenings we would sit on the roof to catch the faintest breath of moving air and watch the children flying kites and dancing. Local children would come and dance for us on the roof top and there would be much innocent fun and laughter. Late at night we would eat together, mountains of rice and curry served on large brass plates with little side dishes. By now I could eat with my fingers without being too clumsy and although I could never sit elegantly, at least by wearing a sari I looked less stiff than I was. I wore a sari because there had been anti-British riots in Calcutta, and once having been mobbed as I biked through the city, it seemed safer to make my allegiance visible. I say mobbed but no harm was done. A student who had seen me and begun shouting "Quit India", the cry taken up by the crowd, then noticed that I was wearing hand spun cloth as my dress was made of *khadi*. This made me instantly recognisable as a follower of Gandhi, and once the student had shouted out this information, the crowd's hostility changed at once to warmth and welcome. My bicycle was returned to me and a little Congress flag tied to the handle-bars. It was illegal to fly the Congress flag at the time and once out of sight and biking down the familiar streets I hastily removed it and then recovered from my ordeal in the India coffee house.

This coffee house was my private retreat near the Centre. It is still there and the greasy, flat omelettes richly flavoured with green chillies are as delicious as ever. I had some conscience pangs about these private orgies of coffee and omelettes as the Quakers allowed one a reasonable allowance for food and in addition a small personal allowance. I never really knew whether to charge these orgies to food or to take them out of the personal allowance. The conscience of a reformed delinquent remains full of holes and I could not settle in my mind what was need as opposed to greed. This type of dilemma does not get easier as I get older. I am always fearfully guilt-ridden when I ponder the Quaker Advices and Queries, a sort of guide to proper Quaker behaviour, one of which reads: "Are you careful not to defraud the public revenue?" Try that one for size next time you fill in your tax form or hop off a bus without paying.

As for saris I do not recommend them for everyday wear in a hot climate. The yards of material tucked in pleats at the waist act as a poultice for prickly heat rash and even one's ankles get chafed with heat and rash, but the Calcutta climate is almost unendurable if one stays there the full year and this combined with tropical infections means one never feels really well, but then neither does anyone else, let alone the children. So I did not mind if I was sometimes overcome with heat exhaustion out on a delivery case and had to recover sitting on the pavement whilst a kind relative gave first aid and fanned me.

I lived with such intensity that nothing could stand in the way of my determination that mothers and babies in "my" area would be properly cared for as if I was personally responsible for preserving life in the face of no matter what destruction. But living at this intensity was fulfilling and all that I could have possibly wanted during the long nursing and midwifery training. India continued to be all I had imagined it would be in spite of the turbulent times. The people were beautiful and Bengal in particular, the home of revolutionaries and poets, suited my temperament. I liked the Bengali volatile and emotional nature unlike most British people who admire the more "macho" northern people of the Punjab. I preferred artists to soldiers, and the creativity of the Bengalis attracted me immensely with their gifts for intimacy and friendship. I felt warmed by it all and adapted easily to the way of life.

Although the work took much of my attention, holidays were obligatory in the Unit, and I set off to explore the subcontinent by bus and train, sometimes with friends and sometimes on my own. These were the days before tourists and the exodus of the young from the West in search of Gurus, so that one could be almost sure of never meeting another European even in the most beautiful and interesting places. I visited all the temple cities in the south, watching with awe and wonder the great flare-lit processions on the days of the great Hindu festivals led by elephants dressed in gold and red cloth carrying the gods dressed in their finery.

I went to Rajputana (now Rajastan) long before the palaces had been robbed of their priceless miniatures and wandered through the mirror-encrusted walls of the Zenana and Ajmer Palace and the pink city of Jaipur. In Udaipur the marble palace still housed the princes, and the palace, the island and the scarlet poinsettias were reflected in the lake. It was still possible then for Indian women to walk in the streets wearing their gold jewellery with no fear of robbery, and it was fashionable for well-off women in the south to be decked in ten or twelve yards of silk saris with four-inch borders of golden threadwork. Poor women wore bright cotton saris and even the poor always managed to look like pictures from some ancient frescoes from Ajanta, the Buddhist caves. It was the timelessness of India that drew me: the long accumulation of culture that makes our own civilisation seem quite crude in comparison.

On one holiday a group of us planned to go trekking into Tibet through Sikkim setting out from Kalimpong. It took months to get the permits through and then we set out on the little railway up through the foothills leaving steaming Calcutta far behind. I was immensely excited, as well one might be, and on the first evening in Kalimpong we looked out on the Himalayas with awe and wonder. But alas that night I was struck down with fever and diarrhoea and although at first I thought I could pretend all was well, it quickly became apparent that I had a serious recurrence of amoebic dysentery. With furious impotence I watched my friends ride away, and knew that it was very unlikely that an opportunity to go into Tibet would ever happen again. I spent the next two weeks in a mission hospital full of leprosy patients, looking out on the snow covered peaks and lamenting. By the end of the second week I was well enough to travel through Sikkim by bus and lorry, through the beautiful land with the ice-blue Teesta river far below in the valley. At Gangtok on the border of Tibet I met up with my companions and we explored this little border town and drank yak butter tea in the dak bungalow. The town was full of Tibetans trading their jewelled knives and ornaments and embroidered cloths. Although I was sad not to have been in Tibet, the ride back through Sikkim was a glorious experience. It took about seven days of intensive trekking, riding our ponies up hill and walking them down. At night we stayed in the dak bungalows and lit log fires and listened to the forest sounds. This was before the days of forest erosion and road building, so our paradise was undisturbed.

CHAPTER SIXTEEN

THE END OF THE RAJ

1946 - 1947

The ominous signs of communal hatred were banking up in the early months of 1946 as the Mountbatten plans for British withdrawal from India were discussed in high places. The Muslims wanted a separate state and no settlement of differences seemed possible. Riots broke out overnight in Calcutta on August 16th 1946 when Jinnah declared a day of direct action, with murderous attacks by Muslims on the Hindu community and vice versa. In the first few days six thousand people died in Calcutta and the dead lay where they had been murdered or were thrust into drains and gutters. Some were taken to the city morgues and that first evening I went with Nihar, a midwifery colleague, to the central morgue to search for her missing brother. We spent hours pulling out the drawers, each containing a pathetic corpse. Fortunately Nihar's brother had escaped and we met up with him later.

Shops were raided and the contents were strewn over the road with glass from broken shop windows. Troops were called in and a general curfew imposed from dusk to dawn. Nihar and I obtained passes so that we could go out at night, but the students had to return to their hospitals. Few people dared to go out in the streets even by day. The problems of food distribution became acute and it was almost impossible to get anyone to hospital as all the rickshaws had vanished and public transport had ceased. A terrible miasma of fear enshrouded the whole city. I was more afraid of the terrified and trigger-happy British and Ghurka soldiers than of any Hindu or Muslim civilian, at least in my own district, which I now knew like the back of my hand.

We continued to deliver babies and were very busy because of the difficulty people had in getting to hospital. We also had to relax our rules and take on cases who had not attended for ante-natal care. We decided we would go to any who were able to send for us as well as continuing to see our own patients as regularly as before, although they could not come to the Centre. No one wanted to risk their lives on the streets. Messages asking us to come were signalled across the roof-tops from one family to another and even though the messages came originally from Muslim areas in the Bazaar, these were conveyed to us by the Hindu families near us. Nor were we hindered when we went about our work which included giving such general relief as we had time for. We took injured people to hospital on hand carts (and at night this was terrifying) and we helped volunteers and the troops remove the dead.

My life was in no particular danger other than from accident, but I continued to be nervous of the British and Ghurka troops. I remember on one occasion asking a young British soldier if he would like to accompany me on a case as it was then past curfew time and he had challenged me. Once off the streets and in the Bazaar the streets were swarming with people and the young man said, as well he might, "There are too many for me", but keeping up a brave front he went with me down the narrow winding alleyways and suddenly found himself in a walled compound where welcoming hands drew him in and he was given a stool to sit on. The children milled around him until their elders called them off. He was given refreshments and Nihar interpreted for him so that for the first time since he had been recruited to Bengal the "nameless hordes" became individuals. He had recently become a father himself so at once at ease he could empathise with what was going on. Fortunately it was a quick delivery and a very much wanted son born to a new Muslim bride, so there was much rejoicing and the young soldier looked at the new-born with such astonished joy that I knew he had shared in a festival that he would never forget.

I was only really badly frightened on one occasion. I had gone on my own at sun-down to Mechua Bazaar to make sure all my patients were all right for the night, carrying my midwifery and first aid kit as usual and a container of dried milk powder in case of need. Walking quietly through the narrow alleyways I suddenly heard the sound of pounding feet. I looked and saw a huge Muslim, wrapped carelessly in a green *lungi* cloth, with staring eyes and a drawn knife. He shouted at me to stop, and this I did without effort being frozen to the spot. Coming near he snatched my bag and said, "Come quickly, my wife's child is about to be born, already her mother says the head can be seen, do not delay". He tucked his knife in his *lungi* (he had probably been using it to slice coconuts when he was sent out to find me); we set off at a run. By the time we arrived at his room the baby was indeed about to be born and a local *dai* was in attendance. Together we helped the mother deliver her baby and later she fed him. The women gathered round and I made up some dried milk solution for the starving family goat.

The unrest in Calcutta lasted a year and when violence flared up again Gandhi began a fast until death unless peace was restored. Suddenly a miracle happened. Muslim and Hindus put aside, at least for the present, their year-long feuds and Gandhi's life was preserved. Calcutta was an amazing sight that day. Gandhi and Suhrawardy, Chief Minister of Bengal, toured the city together and the whole population poured out on to the streets. Hindu embraced Muslim calling each other brothers, poured rose water over each other's hands and rode together in whatever transport was available, crowding trucks and buses, riding three apiece on bicycles, garlanded and joyous, celebrating far into the night. I joined in the celebrations with my colleagues. At last we could all walk through the streets without fear. Order was restored. The night of the long knives at least in Calcutta was over. The troops joined in the celebration using their bayonets to hack open green coconuts.

Although peace was restored to Calcutta unrest had spread to Noakhali in East Bengal and Gandhi, then aged 77, was fasting and walking from village to village to restore peace in a predominantly rural Muslim area rife with hostility. I was able to leave Bela to cope with the Calcutta project and joined Indian Red Cross volunteers and Quaker relief workers to see if we could be of any help to Gandhi.

Gandhi looked serene and strong, not at all the "naked fakir" described at one time by Winston Churchill. I kept in the background but in the evening, after he had his mud pack, Gandhi liked to go for a short walk around the village and I accompanied him, usually walking in the ditch so that his hand could rest on my shoulder. We walked in silence most of the time with Gandhi making an occasional observation about Indian life and the importance of the role of women in village "uplift". He wanted the women to be educated to take proper care of their families and to take part in village affairs.

In the evening there was a gathering of the villagers and I was expected to lead the women in singing one of Gandhi's favourite hymns, "When I survey the wondrous Cross". I knew the words as I had been warned that Gandhi often asked for it to be sung, and the village women did their best to hum an accompaniment.

Gandhi continued his mission in Noakhali and we returned to Calcutta. It was now mid-1946 and I had been scheming and planning for Bela to go to London to train in general nursing as I knew she would not get far with only a midwifery certificate. All her life she had longed to go to England dreaming about it much as I had dreamt of coming to India but her education had suffered from the early death of her father from cholera. I knew I would miss her dreadfully if she went , but I could not deny her the chance to "get on" as I had myself. At last the letter of acceptance came from a London teaching hospital and it was time to part with my dear friend. There was a small problem completing her passport application as she did not know her date of birth but I gave her mine as we were more like sisters and would then be twins.

At about the same time the Midwifery Council in Bengal accepted my plan to include domiciliary midwifery training in the syllabus for midwifery pupils and the first pupils came to the centre to work with me. I recruited a new assistant and we got on with the daily round, running the clinic and delivering babies in both the nearby Hindu area and among the Muslim families in Mechua Bazaar.

Our students, who were usually well educated girls from Christian or very modern Hindu homes were amazed and excited by the conditions they saw. In their application forms they always stated that they wished "to serve our country", but it was unlikely that many or any of them had any previous notion of the poverty on their doorsteps. Some were horrified at the tasks we required of them which broke all caste rules, for example, taking students out on night cases when it was feared they might be attacked by *goondhas* (criminal types), or expecting them to dispose of the placenta.

In hospital many of the "menial tasks" that fell to our lot in the homes would have been done by Harijans (outcasts), but I expected my students to dispose of blood and other body products as if they did not carry any ritual contamination. We would cast the placentas and the soiled dressings into open bins on the way home from a case, and a shower of rats would fly out at the disturbance. I expected too much and on one occasion I was reprimanded for this. I can see that now, but at the time I was totally preoccupied with the task I had set myself, and had no patience with any colleague or student who did not share my passion to bring a first class midwifery service to the poor regardless of personal discomfort and caste restrictions.

So the weeks went by. I missed Bela but got on with the work. There was a clinic in the morning when we tested our patients' blood and urine, examined them for intestinal parasites and arranged, whenever possible, for chest x-rays at the local T.B. centre. We had the services of a visiting doctor who could prescribe treatment for the various ailments that afflicted the women – tuberculosis, malaria and deficiency diseases being the most common. The health visitor students cared for the toddlers and between us we taught the local *dais* and did our best to instil good public health measures in the locality. For the vitamin B deficiencies we taught the families how to sprout gram on damp cloth, and I remember this when I see the bags of sprouting pulses now on sale in health food shops in England! We taught them the advantages of eating unpolished rice with its attendant vitamins as opposed to the gleaming vitamin free white rice preferred by all Bengalis.

By now our work was well accepted. The simple measures we adopted to ensure the safe delivery of the local mothers proved that the recommendations made by Dr. Orkney and Dr. Edwards were easy to implement and stopped the deaths of women in childbirth and the deaths of new-born babies. We worked closely with the local hospitals so that in cases where one might expect obstetric complications the women could be delivered in safety. When no complications were expected the women were safer at home providing one could improve their health in pregnancy and ensure a clean delivery. The dangers of cross infection in hospital was extreme, as it is, to some extent, in British hospitals today.

Faced with the overwhelming poverty and desolate conditions of life there was often very little we could do to improve the health of our patients. Often following a delivery there was no food or drink in the house for the new mother, and we would fetch milk and rice. In spite of the rigorous ante-natal care many of the babies were small at birth or born prematurely.

The climate of Calcutta is as steamy as a Turkish bath for most of the year, but there were occasional chilly nights following the monsoon and there was a problem about how to keep the little new-born warm. There was never more than a cotton cloth or two in the house, and even lying close to the mother did not always give enough warmth to frail new life. Fortunately, I had been sent a large consignment of old fashioned woollen operation socks for distribution, and these, which could not be used for their intended purpose, served wonderfully well to clothe the tiny babies; so with their little faces peeping above the sock cuff, they were able to keep their body warmth and survive.

From time to time I was ill myself. It was impossible to keep well without causing offence to the families we served. One could not always refuse food and drink and many families liked to give us a little feast when the baby was about one month old and order restored to the household. The food was always delicious, but it was inevitable that one caught intestinal infections and parasites. I recovered from these without any long-term effects in spite of the drugs then prescribed which are now known to be dangerous.

Once peace was restored I was less fraught because it was possible to have students out again and to employ another trained midwife to supervise them. I wanted to be sure I could pass on a flourishing service when I left as it was nearing the second half of my final year. I became less fanatical about doing everything myself and began delegating most of the routine work. This released more emotional energy and I became aware of a very strong attraction for an American working in another relief agency whom I met in Puri, a seaside retreat near the great temple of Jaganath on the Orissa coast. It was only a short distance from Calcutta, and I spent a weekend there when I was recovering from another bout of dysentery. Harry was staying in the same hotel and we swam together in the tumultuous seas and went on an expedition to Konarak, the sun temple known as the Black Pagoda. I did not know about this temple and I had retained a curious innocence or ignorance about love. I was not expecting to see such a magnificent erotic work of art. I had some knowledge about Hinduism but I did not know about these sculptures and all their amazing beauty came as a complete surprise. Harry did not share my cultural ignorance but we both found the temple carvings overwhelming. The symbolic meaning is religious but the erotic impact of the carvings which portray the sexual act in every conceivable form acted on me as an overpowering aphrodisiac.

I was nearly twenty-seven then and had not experienced heterosexual love, but with Harry, who shared all my ideals and passions for India, I had found the perfect lover. He was quite shocked to find I was a virgin but I was less shocked to learn he was married and responded to him without moral qualms. After that weekend we met whenever we could in Calcutta. Harry's time in India was drawing to a close and we did not know when we would meet again. I had already planned to follow him to America but we knew a period of separation was inevitable. I settled quite quickly into the role of the "other woman" and did not care at all that we could never be free to marry. Marriage was not on my hidden life agenda and I never wanted children. I told Harry of my homosexual lovers in the past and his only response was, "You are all that any man could desire" and he could not imagine how any man could be jealous of love between women which he did not perceive as a threat.

Harry was not only a romantic lover in the great American tradition but also very protective and no doubt fulfilled my need for fathering, so that I felt immensely secure in his love and continued to feel so for many years. He was considerably older than I was, more experienced in the world, very responsible and kind. The fact that he was deceiving his wife did not concern me much then. I knew that he would never be able to leave her, that she was not in good health and that I fulfilled a need in his life that she could not meet. My moral development was distinctly primitive.

To the background of this glorious and unscrupulous love affair I continued my work, but I began to consider the future and came to the conclusion that I should study public health nursing before venturing on to the next stage of my career. One day I read an article about the Frontier Nursing Service in Kentucky, a horseback nursing service to the mountain people in the Appalachian Mountains. It did not take more than an instant for me to recognise that this was the ideal job combining adventure, a restorative period in a healthy environment and the possibility of being near my loved one. I wrote to the service who replied, "Although you do not ride or drive, we would be happy to accept you for a two year contract when you are ready to come". I still thought it would be a good idea to take the health visitor course first as I assumed my career would continue in developing countries, and that such a qualification would be of value, so I was glad to hear that I had been accepted by the Royal College of Nursing to begin in October 1947 on my return from India.

Harry left and I continued for a while in Calcutta, but with the onset of the monsoon I began to feel very ill. During the monsoon the streets were always flooded and I could not protect my feet as I waded in about a foot of water and the debris of food and filth floated by. I thought I had dysentery as I was quite accustomed to feeling ill from time to time, but then my fever mounted and I went up to the Unit where the American doctor looked quite concerned because he could find no parasites in my blood or other infection. He said benignly that he could be sure of one thing, that I had not got Rocky Mountain Spotted Fever, but "goodness knows what you have got" and I was sent to bed with prophylactic doses of penicillin. As the days went by I grew progressively jaundiced. I felt I was dying which made me intensely angry. I had caught leptospiral jaundice, commonly known as Weil's disease, which is spread by sewer rats in contaminated water. I was very ill for some weeks and for a time it did seem that I might die. I remember the marvellously restorative effect of saline infusions which stopped the vomiting but I surveyed my orange skin with some dismay. Once I recovered it was decided I should go to Darjeeling to convalesce and then return to England a few weeks before my contract ended. I was by now somewhat skeletal and there did not seem much sense in returning to work in Sitaram Ghosh Street. The midwifery service was now well established and I could leave it with some confidence that the work would go on well.

It was cold in Darjeeling and shrouded in mist. Lying in bed one morning I looked up and saw above the clouds the snow capped peak of Kanchanjunga with its base shrouded in mist. It was an awesome sight.

I went for walks and long pony rides through the forest and quickly recovered my health. Back in the hotel I wrote letters to dear Harry now in New York. He thought the idea of my joining the Kentucky Frontier Nursing Service quite splendid, as indeed did I.

My last few weeks in Calcutta were spent in Sitaram Ghosh Street with a series of farewell parties and loving encounters with students and patients. I promised to write, I promised to come back, I promised never to forget them. Then on August 15th, 1947, Indian Independence Day, I left Calcutta for Bombay and the homeward journey. The Indian flag so long banned was flying in every village and there were cheering crowds celebrating. Independence had been achieved at last. Congress was in power. The last days of the Raj were completed.

Harry 1949

Joan and Harry 1949

CHAPTER SEVENTEEN

KENSINGTON

1948-1949

The health visitor course began soon after I returned to London from Calcutta. I found a room in Edith Grove, Chelsea and adjusted as best I could to the cultural shock of being back in England with winter drawing in. I did not feel particularly well. Fortunately Bela, my Bengali friend and colleague was still in training so we could be homesick for India together, but the transition was not easy and I was glad to have the opportunity to study again rather than have to rush straight into a job. Plunging into academic work is a useful and productive way of bridging a change of direction, and I was to use this device increasingly as I grew older, usually rationalising it in some way. In my heart I did not need to learn about public health but I did need "time out".

A year later I qualified. I was required by the terms of my grant to work as a health visitor for a year, and I was quite glad to consolidate the training. It was then 1948, the year the National Health Service came into being, and we worked towards what was then known as the "appointed day". Until then women and children especially were hard put to get any necessary medical care unless they were rich enough to afford private treatment. The coming of the N.H.S. meant they could get their varicose veins and gynaecological problems seen to and the financial burden and fear of being ill was alleviated.

I was appointed to work in North London with colleagues in a central maternity and child welfare clinic. We each covered part of the district and knew all the families on our "patch". There were no Children's Departments then, nor of course Social Services departments. Health visitors supervised day nurseries, daily minders and foster parents, and assessed potential adoptive parents. I enjoyed this part of the work as it involved more psychological understanding than the usual duties. I was rather bored with routine immunisation and "baby" clinics. My personal background and training inclined me more towards acute clinical work with maximum responsibility, and to working with families with complicated psychological problems, although as yet I had no training in social welfare.

Sometimes our work with families brought us into contact with the N.S.P.C.C. Inspectors (who at that time wore uniform) but it was before the days anyone recognised "battered babies" and the word incest was barely whispered. Many of the children in our case-load were neglected because their parents lived in dire poverty in overcrowded slum flats and houses, and in such circumstances physical neglect and mental cruelty to children were not problems we felt able to do much about, though on occasions we shared concerns with the local "cruelty man" who would then investigate.

Large families were more common than they are now, and family planning clinics existed, supported by a voluntary agency, but only married women were accepted for treatment, at least officially. The clinics tended to be secreted modestly in side streets and were still considered quite a pioneering venture. Single women who could afford it went to private practitioners, the fee for a nurse I remember was £5.00 and I recall feeling very modern and adult when I was fitted with my first Dutch Cap as part of my preparation for going to America. There was no "Pill" in those days, thank goodness, so birth control was not a health hazard.

Health visitors worked in close co-operation with the local hospital and I remember my first contact with a medical social worker (then called a lady almoner) at St. Charles' Hospital. She had asked me to consult with her about plans for an unmarried mother who was on my case-load and I was impressed by the almoner's manner, the attentive way she listened, her quiet unmoralistic understanding of the girl's problem. I made a mental note that the social work approach to patients differed from the more usual authoritative stance of doctors and nurses. Perhaps, I thought, social workers do not always assume they know what is best for people, unlike many of my medical and nursing colleagues.

As soon as my year's service was nearly completed I finalised plans to join the Kentucky Frontier Nursing Service. Once more there were partings and farewell parties and the sorrow of leaving dear friends combined with the excitement of a new venture. It was once more time to go "walk about". The pattern of my career has meant that I have had more than my fair share of farewell parties. This time I was seen off from Waterloo Station by my nice colleagues en route for Southampton where I boarded the Ile de France, a very comfortable and luxurious small liner which, because of heavy seas, took seven days to cross the Atlantic. I love the sea and the extended time gave me the opportunity to think about all that lay ahead, as far as I could envisage. It was all very well to be a romantic, I thought, dreaming of riding horseback up the trails – but I had never ridden a horse and had no experience of even living in the country. But I did not really doubt my ability to cope.

In New York I was met by Harry and we had a wonderful week at the Gramercy Park Hotel, exploring the city and delighting in the first long period we had spent together. At the end of the week, all too short a "honeymoon" really, Harry saw me off in the first of a series of Greyhound buses to Kentucky.

CHAPTER EIGHTEEN

KENTUCKY - WINTER

1949-1950

My first impression of the Appalachian Mountains was of tree-covered brown hills shrouded in mist with winding dirt roads climbing up between little towns, each looking rather like a film set, with the local stores, central jail and wooden houses with their balconies. I arrived in Wendover, at the administrative headquarters of the Frontier Nursing Service and was welcomed by Mrs Breckenridge, the director, and some of the nurses who worked in the nearby Frontier Nursing Hospital at Hyden. There were three or four beautifully built log houses in Wendover, used as homes and offices, a few barns, and below the dirt road the rushing Red Bird river. I noted the swinging bridge across it and wondered how I would ever dare to use it.

Mrs Breckenridge's family had lived in Kentucky for generations and was very respected and influential. Following the death of her two children and her husband she decided to train as a nurse-midwife and see what she could give for the poor mountain people who were without any medical service. She trained as a nurse in America and then as a midwife in Scotland with the Islands and Highlands Service to prepare herself for a pioneering enterprise which was to become world renowned. She first set about researching the needs of the mountain families; then raised money in all the great cities of America, setting up medical and nursing committees who would help to lay down practical guidelines for nurse-midwives working under such isolated, geographically remote conditions, far from medical help.

The medical boards approved procedures and set these out in manuals which became the "standing orders" for generations of nurse-midwives employed by the Service, and which were regularly updated in the light of current medical knowledge. They not only covered every aspect of caring for midwifery patients so that in any emergency the midwife knew what to do, but also authorised her, in the absence of a doctor, to give the necessary treatment for common ailments such as pneumonia and the infections of childhood.

Mrs Breckenridge recruited nurse-midwives from both America and England, and in time established a small hospital on the spur of Thousand Sticks Mountain, in Clay County, with outpost nursing centres and later a training school for midwife students who came from all over the country and abroad for the unique experience of training and working in a rural project which gave the mountain people a first class health service. By 1962 (twelve years after my time in the service) 10,000 babies had been delivered by the Frontier Nursing Service and the mortality rate compared favourably with that in New York.

There were few roads then and the nurses rode horseback along the mountain trails to their patients, across rivers and up the creeks, at first accompanied by couriers, young city girls who paid to act as volunteers during college vacations, helping new recruits, keeping the trails open, whitewashing the barns and doing other useful chores. It was rumoured that American families put their daughters down as volunteers as soon as they were born, rather like some British families book a place for their sons at Eton. The Service had become over the years a symbol to the American people of all the values they held most dear – enterprise, rugged independence, valour and hard work. Perhaps the most startling success, due entirely to Mrs Breckenridge's persuasive diplomacy and administrative genius, is that the medical profession gave the Service their blessing and support so that the nurse-midwives could give necessary drugs to their patients and carry out emergency procedures normally performed by doctors. I have worked in other areas of the world where it has been virtually impossible to persuade doctors to sanction midwives (even under strict regulation) to administer life saving drugs to their patients, even though geographic conditions made it impossible to get the patient to hospital had they been in a fit state to travel .

On my first night in Kentucky I sat drinking sherry with the other nurses (Mrs Breckenridge's idea of a glass of sherry was half a silver tankard full for each nurse) in front of a blazing log fire, feeling very much a townie in my city clothes and nylons. My future colleagues wore blue uniforms, jodhpurs, jackets, white shirts, black ties and high black mountaineer laced boots. I felt at the edge of a whole new mysterious way of life. Jean Hollins, the saintly woman, who acted as "vet" to all the animals sat nursing a sick cat on her lap. Yards of rubber tubing and a funnel were draped on the back of her chair as she had just come in from administering first aid to a local farmer's cow. It was Jean who acted as farrier, midwife to the cows, and who visited the outpost nurses each month to deliver foodstuffs, shoe the horses and generally check up on animal welfare. I listened to the talk, fascinated, but bewildered: it was all about horses, local events and the state of the mountain trails now winter was settling in. I retired early to bed – there was a log fire burning in the grate, the oil lamp burnt peacefully and I laughed knowing that I had once again flung myself in at the deep end, from some innate need for adventure, challenge and change.

The next day I was instructed to go round with the couriers, and be shown the hospital, the barns, the horses and some of the trails. One of the girls taught me to drive a jeep and within a week or two I took my driving test. It was well known that no nurse had ever been failed. We backed out of the shed and I asked my instructor which way I should go. "Which ever way you like", he said. This was fortunate as I had no idea when I turned the wheel in which direction I would be facing, and we chugged off through Hyden. There was one alarming moment when the sheriff stepped out from the bar and walked across the street and my instructor thought, quite rightly, that any moment I would run him down, but fortunately this tragedy was averted, and after a brief drive up the hills and down back into Hyden I was told that I could have my licence.

A few days later I went to sit the examination for the Kentucky Midwives Board as I had to be registered in the state. This was an interesting experience as it was quite apparent that the young examiner was accustomed to examining obstetrics medical students, not midwives. "Sit down Joan," he said, "What do you think this is?" and passed over the table a cup of coffee in one hand and a bottle with some indescribable specimen in it. Fortunately, I instantly recognised it as a hydatidiform mole, a form of uterine cancer. We discussed this at some length and the proper treatment for the condition. I was then given a true and false question paper to answer and did not find this an arduous exercise, though I knew I would lose a mark by answering "Yes" to the question, "Is painless labour possible?", as Americans did not recognise "natural" childbirth at this time.

I stayed six weeks in Wendover and Hyden. I had to learn how to groom and I was told to practice on Tenacity, the mule used for carrying logs up to Wendover. Dear creature, I crooned over her as I brushed her front fringe and removed the odd corn seed from her ears. It's fitting, I thought, that my first friend in the service should be a mule. Then I was promoted to grooming horses, but I still made Tenacity my first morning task, warming my icy hands on her firm woolly belly. She reminded me of a childhood toy in the nursery at Parsonage Farm, a stuffed donkey on wheels for whom I had an inordinate affection.

Down in the great barns at Hyden below the hospital, I met the beautiful service horses used by the nurses in the area. One day I found two small kittens there, Ferdinand and Isabel, so small that each could curl up on a hand. They had been rescued by a nurse who discovered them under her jeep and we were told that they would have to learn to be barn cats, and that we must not be sentimental. Their job was to catch the rats, all of whom, like Samuel Whiskers, were ten times bigger than they were. A friend and I decided to intervene and organise a rescue party. The kittens co-operated fully by jumping the six feet or so from the barn loft into the coat which I held out for them. Then we put them in cotton bags, known as pokes locally, buttoned them under our jackets for warmth, and raced them back to Hyden where we had arranged that Hiram would give them a home in his grocery store. His two little boys were delighted and so they were soon happily settled. I knew they could not survive as barn cats and I was glad we had committed this felony.

"Brownie" the Assistant Director told me that although I had my licence to drive a jeep and could do so in emergencies, it was apparent that my driving was not up to the standard required in the service, but that I would be taught to change wheels and do elementary mechanical repairs in case I was ever stuck with them. Meanwhile I was instructed in horse riding, and although I had not ridden before I fell in love with the whole idea and was so thrilled to be riding that I quickly learnt enough skills to be allocated an outpost district, Flat Creek on the banks of the Red Bird river. I was glad about this as I did not really enjoy staying in Hyden and Wendover. I wanted to get out to the deeper country.

By the time I arrived at Flat Creek it was deep winter, the muddy brown river had changed to a milky green and the red Cardinal birds were swooping across the water. Flat Creek Centre consisted of a well-built three-bedroomed log house situated above the barns with a creek running through the pastures, about five minutes away from the local store and chapel. The river ran close to the house past the store and I was to have many rides along its banks. It was envisaged that I would look after Flat Creek Centre while the regular nurse, Stevie, was on six months leave, and there was a period of about two or three weeks before Stevie left to enable me to become orientated to the work and the district.

Our household consisted of Janie, a fifteen year old maid, who lived in the Centre and looked after us and only went home on Sundays. We were required to have a maid if for no other reason than to milk the precious Jersey cow, but Janie also cooked and kept house for us, and was a delight to have around the house. Two horses were allocated to Flat Creek Centre. Doc was a sixteen-hand dark bay, younger than Rex , powerful, good natured and very gentle. Rex, whom I thought of as henna-coloured, was irritable and fiery, and really did not like anyone riding him except Stevie. The horses were groomed in the morning by our stable girl Elsie, aged eighty, who had inherited the job when her father died. She was five foot three in height and weighed about seven stone. Sometimes Doc looked down on her with some consternation as she cradled his hooves to clean them out one by one, as if he wondered whether she had the strength. Elsie could do anything with the horses, and I would watch her as she stood on a log crooning to Doc combing his beautiful thick black mane.

The nurses groomed the horses at night and on Sundays. It was never possible to have a "lie in" on Sundays because Doc and Rex would thunder with their hooves in the stable demanding attention – they wanted their breakfast and then the joy of being let loose in the field all day. If one of our patients was inconsiderate enough to go into labour on Sunday it was no easy task to catch and saddle one of the horses. Grooming was a job I dearly loved, even at the end of a long day. In the winter it was a fairly simple matter, just rubbing and drying, then brushing off the caked mud when it dried. But in the summer we washed our horses down with water from the creek, bucket after bucket, then gave them a quick rub down in the sun – but Doc (who became "my" horse whom I rode every day except in emergency) liked to follow his bath with a quick roll in the dust, waving his hooves in the air, and it gave him such joy I seldom stopped him even though further grooming became a real labour of love.

The two cats, Sandy and Butch, were marmalade and white. Butch was a great rat catcher and he would sometimes come out of the barn with two dead rats held by their tails in his mouth. He would fancy a new laid egg on occasion, and help himself – from the horse food trough where they were often conveniently laid. He was also a great tease – hiding in the barn at night so that when I had groomed, fed and bedded down the horses and locked the barn I could hear a pathetic miaow as I trudged up the slope to the house, carrying the heavy saddle bags, and there was Butch at the hay-loft window, demanding to be rescued.

The remaining domestic pet was Blondie, a perky white dog who went everywhere with us, trotting gamely beside the horses and swimming across the rivers, except when it was too deep when she was lifted up on the saddle.

I found the first few weeks fairly tough going as it was bitterly cold, and we started work early. We held a clinic twice a week in the house between 8.30 am and 9.30 am, giving routine treatment for minor ailments, "worming" the children and giving immunisations and first aid. I remember once treating a miner's quite badly injured finger and when he did not come back I visited him at home to make sure he did not need hospital treatment. He greeted me cheerfully, saying "I didn't like to bother you 'uns because it fell off ok" showing me his stump. When we finished the clinic we would carry our leather saddle bags of nursing equipment down to the barn (having checked and restocked them the evening before) where Elsie would be waiting with both horses saddled and ready. We mounted, tightened the girths and rode off.

Each outpost centre nurse cared for approximately a hundred families in a five mile radius, and this could involve quite a lot of riding when cases were at different ends of the district. A typical day's work might involve two or three post-natal visits, an ante-natal visit to a mother who was too far advanced in pregnancy to ride to the clinic herself, several visits to treat patients with chest infections and routine visits with chronic ailments such as cancer. If a patient went into labour all other visits had to be postponed, of course.

When we were not busy we would attempt more public health work, taking well-water specimens to send to the Hyden Hospital, and giving such advice as we could on child care. The earth closet latrines contaminated the subsoil and as they were usually at a higher ground level than the shallow wells the water was unfit to drink, but the families could not be persuaded to boil it. Fortunately most adults drank very little water, preferring coffee or moonshine, but the children were chronically infested with parasites.

Our patients lived in log homes along the creeks usually about a mile apart, far from the dirt track roads, across the river and over the passes. The shacks, for most were little more than this, usually consisted of one or two rooms with perhaps a small kitchen attached. The walls were pasted with newspaper and magazine covers giving a patchwork effect. There were guns above the mantelpiece, and usually an improving text such as "Love your mother, honour the Lord" alongside. A black wood and coal burning stove was a central fixture. Beautiful patchwork quilts, which would be worth a fortune in England now, draped the beds, and each spring these would be washed in the creek and hung over the bushes to dry. As there was little space to spare for storage, bottled fruit was kept under the bed and sweet potatoes piled in a corner. Chickens often squawked around the home and we would make sure there were no eggs on the bed before examining our patients. There was no running water and of course no electricity. At night we delivered the babies by lamp and torch light, and sometimes in very poor homes it was so cold that our forceps froze in their dish. We washed our rubber sheets and instruments in the creek before re-packing them in the saddle bags.

Once Stevie was confident that I could manage Doc she let me go on visits on my own and I loved the silence and isolation, the sound of rain in the trees and the cascading creeks. Storms could be quite exciting and one would have to ride carefully holding the reins steady and close in case the horse was alarmed by a cracking branch. The moss along the creek side was brilliant green and near to habitation pigs and chickens rustled amongst the leaves. I watched entranced as dear Doc's careful hooves trod delicately amongst the rocks. In the valleys the marsh grass looked salmon pink in the wintry light and the corn stalks crackled in the wind. Icicles over three or four feet long hung from the boulders. Some of our patients lived high up in the hills with the river twisting far below. There were waterfalls everywhere and still a few pale golden leaves on the beech trees. Hiawatha country! Shades of another dream of my childhood. Blondie, the little white dog would trot beside me shaking herself and you could hear the tinkle of the ice bells in her coat. When we went into the cabins the patients would say, "your old hound she's a-suffering bad, bring her near the fire, bring her close to the fire," and Blondie would curl up and lick herself and recover.

That first winter there were many cases of pneumonia and of mumps. The latter caused terrible complications in the men, and I was busy distributing cloth slings for them to use to suspend their inflamed testicles. The children's main illnesses were intestinal infestation and measles. They loved the nurse to visit and would try to bribe me to call by saying they would play the guitar and sing a song. Some of them went to school but in the spring they helped with the farming. The schools were one-roomed white shacks down in the valleys and quite a few returning G.I.'s, adult men, attended school too. Many of them could not get work in the local coal mines or scratch a living from farming, so drew what was called "rocking chair money", state assistance. The children and men alike carried a lard can of food for the day.

Most of our patients were young, but there were a few prematurely old people, particularly women, and I remember Cora sitting on her porch panting for dear life, desperately ill in the last stages of cancer. I had to take her to hospital and as I led her out to the jeep, (she lived near the dirt road), Flora, her granddaughter, aged six, whispered to me, "I know what's the matter with Gran, she a-swearing herself to death and it's choking her". Cora spat tobacco and when she was first admitted to hospital the doctor thought this was rusty sputum caused by her disease. All the children chewed tobacco too, and when I once remarked upon the dangers of this habit they told me that I knew nothing about it and should try it – I did, and did not progress very far, but managed to spit it out into the fire with a degree of accuracy which earned applause.

I was quite frequently called out at night. The Service regulation was that if the patient's husband could get to us at night, we could go to the case but he must accompany us. On the whole the mountaineers, who were afraid of witches, preferred to fetch the nurse in the daytime. But we did have some night calls and I loved riding in the dark. We were not supposed to return home on our own until dawn, though I often did, anxious to get some rest for the horses and myself. When the baby was born the family cooked a breakfast of biscuits (scones in English) with gravy and coffee, cornbread and bacon and white sour butter, potatoes and green beans. A very different diet from the vegetarian one I had temporarily given up when I returned from India.

Riding back on Doc through the cornfields we would sometimes go faster than we were supposed to, Doc snatching corn as we sped by. There was very expensive equipment in our saddle bags and the horses had been trained to a running walk which did not jog the equipment, but sometimes we dared to go rather faster. Doc would know his way home so we were never lost. When we were near Flat Creek Doc would whinny and far below Rex would answer though I could not hear him. Back in the barn my feet were sometimes so frozen to the wooden stirrups that I would have to knock them out, and then dismount stiffly, before taking off Doc's saddle and bridle, giving him a quick rub down and covering him with a blanket. Once Doc was groomed, fed and munching contentedly in his stall it was good to be welcomed home by Janie, who would have the log fire burning cheerfully, the oil lamps lit and supper ready.

I grew very attached to Janie and missed her on her day off. She could not read or write and I would draft love letters for her and she would sing: "I will cling to my man with his waving black hair but I am longing to go to the long shadowed grove then I'll meet my darling, my darling, my own", a song she was very partial to from Wild Wood Flower by Mary Bell Carter. We would also practise Moody and Sankey hymns in the evening as it was customary for the Frontier Nurse to sing the solo hymn at all weddings at the local chapel and Janie would rehearse me for these occasions.

There was a pleasant contrast between the rigours of the working days and the comforts of home. The furnace in the basement belched hot air through vents into the living and bedrooms and we had an endless supply of logs from local families who would barter them for manure which we kept under the porch. Sometimes I would go out at night to replenish our stock and meet the barn owl perched on the low roof. Before dark I would chase up the ducks (which nurses kept as pets) and push them safely into their hutches so they would not float down the creek and be caught by one of the Sizemoore family for dinner. They were easier to catch than the hens, some of whom roosted with the horses in the barn but at night I tried to get them all into their own house. Alas, when Stevie went on leave a few hens died during the winter and local people told me that they must have been bitten by rattle-snakes which were common in the area. When Jean came round to shoe the horses she told me that I should have been giving them grit as with the ground frozen it was difficult for them to peck it up themselves.

I had a marvellous sense of freedom and responsibility when I took over full responsibility for the district, and I hoped to manage better than Stevie imagined I would! Understandably she had doubts about my ability to take care of everything and all the creatures properly, as I had never worked in a rural area and was ignorant about country ways. Most of the nurses in the Service came from the country and were accustomed to riding and hunting or had experience in animal care before they joined the Service. But I comforted Stevie by writing her long and regular letters when she was in England, giving her weekly bulletins about the beloved animals, especially her favourites, her horse Rex and the little dog Blondie.

Once I was foolish enough to harness Doc to the balcony of a homestead instead of to a fence or tree while I went inside to give a morphia injection to a lady with cancer. Something must have frightened Doc because he jumped and tugged and the whole little cabin fell down; fortunately not injuring anyone. My patient Cassie's husband said "Don't you worry nurse, if your old horse can pull it down I can raise it up again," and he soon did.

I never really learnt to cope with cleaning the horse tackle down in the barn – it was too cold and I must have been the only nurse in the service who brought it into the kitchen to do. The wonderful smell of leather soap added to the Sunday aroma of scones baking in the wood burning stove. Once all this was out of the way another Sunday task was to check all the midwifery and nursing equipment, and there was sterilising to be done in the immense pressure cooker which belched steam in a most alarming manner. Before dark the oil lamps had to be trimmed and cleaned. On Sundays Janie drifted off in a little boat across the river and I hoped the river would not be too high for her to get back in time to milk Dulcie. When she returned we would talk about the day's events and churn the butter and I would cook supper for us both before we settled down by the fire to gossip.

During that first winter there was an epidemic of cat 'flu and dear Butch, the big marmalade cat, caught it severely and after a day or two he vanished from the house. I thought he had gone somewhere quiet to die and it was not until a week later, one Sunday afternoon, that I heard a pathetic miaow and there was Butch, a shadow of his former self, rubbing against the refrigerator demanding milk. He must have been hiding among the pipes in the basement. Soon he was back to his normal rat-catching, egg-stealing self.

The nurses were expected to help any sick local animals as best we could, though if an animal was really ill an attempt would be made to get it to Hyden. But we gave simple treatment to cows with mastitis and the annual rabies inoculations to dogs and cats. If one of our horses or the cow was at all unwell we would send an urgent message to Hyden and Jean would drive over at once. The standard of horse care in the Service was second to none and we had yet another instruction manual to guide us on their daily care and on elementary nursing, taking temperatures etc. No horse ever got a saddle sore as we unsaddled each time we stopped to make a nursing call and groomed the horses meticulously.

I had one patient I shall never forget, Elijah, aged seventy-five with silvery grey hair and a hooked nose. Both his grandparents came from Scotland, as did many of the local families, and he could remember his mother talking Gaelic. He was very ill with a lung abscess and advanced cardiac disease and I knew that he would not live. All his relatives had been summoned to his bedside. Over the last fifty years he had worked in the mines and had only recently given up work. Gathered around him were numerous members of his family and about twelve children. The beds were covered with sleeping babies and the kitchen full of women cooking – all fine, large, handsome women with hooked noses like Elijah. The women looked after each other's babies indiscriminately, changing and bathing them, and only when it came to feeding them at the breast did they clasp their own. The youngest of the grandchildren was only ten days old, a lusty boy greatly admired by his grandfather. Elijah told his son that he did not want a "brought on" (factory made) coffin, and so a very splendid one was prepared for him out of poplar wood and lined with satin. He approved this and died peacefully a few days later.

The religion of most of the mountaineer families included talking in tongues and handling snakes, but when it came to weddings and funerals, most elected to go to the local chapel which was strongly Methodist – hence the Moody and Sankey hymns. Elijah's funeral was attended not only by his extensive family, but by all the families in the valley and it was a most moving occasion.

During that severe winter I had a telegram to say my mother had died. Later I had a letter explaining that she had been found dead in the kitchen with a cup of cold tea on the arm of her chair. She may have felt a bit weak and thought "oh dear, I'll make a cuppa". The post mortem report revealed that she had extensive cardiac and lung disease, so she must have been ill for a long time, as I had always suspected, but I was always glad I hadn't pushed her into going to hospital which she so dreaded. My last memories of her were of going for a walk on a hot summer day. She saw a horse plagued with flies and climbed over the barbed wire and under a hedge to dab its head with lavender oil. During my last visit her appalling pet cat, Felix, of indefinite age, with a missing paw, grey fur with bare scurfy patches and most of his ears missing, jumped on to my lap and purred in a rusty contralto. I was glad to hear that Felix was found in the kitchen with her so that she did not die unattended.

The big barn, Hyden 1949

Mrs Breckenridge with Dobbin

Joan and Dobbin July 1950
Hyden, Kentucky

Joan and Doc

Doc

Joan seen through Doc's ears

Cassie and family

Cassie's children with Doc

Bull Creek Clinic
Clay County, Kentucky

Kentucky home
Slightly above average standard

CHAPTER NINETEEN

KENTUCKY - SPRING

1950

Eventually the long Kentucky winter ended – it was said to be the worst winter in living memory – wherever one goes this seems to happen! Spring in April 1950 was beautiful. There were numerous turquoise blue and black striped butterflies, black ones with blue edging, and brilliant yellow ones with a black border, which fluttered around the horses' legs. The red-bud tree with its purple blossom was in bloom. Then the dogwood trees blossomed layer upon layer of four-petalled blossom that looked like massed roses as one looked down on them from the hill tops. It was a Frontier Nursing Service tradition that nurses who perhaps only intended to come for a year or two stayed on and on year after year waiting to see the dogwood blossom once again.

Early in the spring the local families were busy putting in seed potatoes and ploughing the hills with mules and wooden implements. Behind the plough walked the barefooted children scattering fertilizer from a bucket or lard can. A few peach trees and apples were in blossom and water snakes glided in the creeks, little turtles hid under the rocks, frogs were beginning to spawn in the puddles alongside Flat Creek and lizards raced across the road. In the woods azaleas bloomed and on nursing visits the children gave me roses to pin in my hair.

We had an unexpected heat-wave that spring and I rode without a coat with shirt sleeves rolled up. It was lovely coming into the barn from the sunshine, all cool and white and deserted except for hens perched on the stalls who fluttered when we entered and made quite a commotion before escaping through the windows. The two cats would be curled asleep on the sacks in the grain room recovering from their night's adventures. But then the brief summer ceased and there was pouring rain and I was constantly drenched and steaming in front of the fire in the patients' log cabins, and on the way home Doc would pick his way carefully down the creek through the swirling waters.

Nurses had long weekends off every six weeks and a relief nurse would take over. On these weekends I usually met Harry in a Kentucky town and we would drive from place to place exploring the country, staying at motels and having a joyous and companionable time. Sometimes he came to Flat Creek for a weekend, and he taught me how to cook, using spices and garlic, tasting the food and encouraging me. When we were not together we wrote each other long and detailed letters and this letter writing often occupied the evening while Janie whistled over the washing up and the lamplight flickered.

Through the long spring and summer days Doc and I went on our rounds and I grew to love him inordinately, my faithful partner on the mountain trails. At midday we would usually stop for a picnic under the trees and Doc would nuzzle me for his apple and boiled sweet. He would be very put out every time our schedule of visits changed, as change they did, and resist passing a homestead we had previously been visiting regularly. I would try to explain to him as he twitched his ears crossly about the complications of the job. I only rode Rex occasionally, just to give him exercise, and he seemed quite content enough to browse the day away in the field and to welcome back his stable mate in the evening. When I did ride him I could feel his irritability and I knew he missed Stevie. Once he stepped just a little too close to the edge of the river as we rode back from the store where I had bought the week's supply of provisions. The river was not deep, but we floundered in and the bread and other provisions floated downstream. Janie, returning from a visit to her family, saw the accident and became quite hysterical, "I thought you would be killed dead for sartin" she lamented, laughing and sobbing as Rex and I tried to recover our dignity.

Although the Frontier nurse-midwives carried great responsibility in caring for families in such a remote area the traditions and the spirit of the Service was such that one felt immensely supported and not often unduly alarmed. If a patient was seriously ill or did not respond to treatment it was always possible to send for a doctor from Hyden Hospital or in some circumstances to get the patient there by mule and jeep. The journey took about three hours – so unless it was an acute emergency one knew that medical help was near at hand. But when an acute emergency did arise it could be very worrying indeed. One morning I was called out early to a woman who was bleeding heavily from an incomplete miscarriage. I gave her the prescribed treatment but the bleeding continued and it was obvious that she needed surgical intervention in hospital. My fear was that she would bleed to death before we got there, and she nearly did. Local people were accustomed to responding quickly in emergencies and within minutes the children had rounded up all the neighbouring able-bodied men and we carried the patient on her bed down the creek to the road. It was too far to go home to fetch the jeep, but fortunately a coal lorry came by, stopped at once and we heaved the bed on to the back and sped to Hyden. The patient survived after massive transfusions and I was glad to see her at home a few weeks later, apparently unperturbed by her dreadful experience, calmly bottling fruit with her children around her helping. She apologised for having given us "so much trouble" and added "I guess I was apunishin bad that day, but praise the Lord I didn't die, with all my sins upon me."

As summer drew to a close I began to ponder about my future. My original contract with the Service was only for a year, but this had been extended when Stevie wrote to ask for a longer period of leave to settle things at her home and I was quite happy to stay on until the Fall. Once Stevie came back she would of course take over the Centre again and although if I had wanted to stay on in Kentucky there would have been other work to do I could not imagine taking root in another district, leaving Janie and all the beloved animals. It would be easier to go somewhere quite different. My plan had been to gain rural experience and return to India or to some other "developing" nation, but I had no clear idea how this plan could be realised. Mrs Breckenridge asked if I would like to go to Guam where a midwife was needed to start a service, but I could not see myself working in a naval base. Then there was Harry, and all that relationship meant in pleasure and conflict.

As so often happens, fate took a hand. Harry's poor wife found out he was having an "affair" and was not unnaturally distraught with grief. Harry wrote to tell me about this and I knew I should back out from the relationship and that if I did so his marriage would survive.

At about the same time, actually almost by the same post, came an offer of a job from the World Health Organisation. A midwifery adviser was needed to join a team in Lahore who were setting up a project to train community nurses. The team was led by none other than Dr Jean Orkney, whose work had inspired me so many years ago. I cabled for more details of the job to give myself time to reflect, but in fact my mind had already made itself up. Pakistan was less dear to my heart than India, but the job itself sounded interesting, and I was also thrilled to be offered work with the U.N. with all that implied at the time in idealism and challenge.

Soon Stevie returned to Flat Creek and there was a great celebration. Rex nuzzled her rapturously and Blondie hovered on her hind legs ecstatic with joy. Stevie and I rode round the district, she to renew her friendships and me to take my farewells. I was touched by the affection shown by the families and knew it would be hard to leave them and the Service, and indeed the whole experience of working in the mountain community had been a privilege I would never forget. One family gave me as a memento the rattles from a dead rattlesnake that rustled ominously on their string! "So you'll remember the Mountains, nurse, when you are far away."

The most difficult parting was of course from dear Doc. I went to the barn for the last time to feed him his favourite boiled sweets and hug his dark head and feel his warm neck under the thick mane. It was heartbreaking. Then Harry arrived, we loaded up the car and started on the long journey to New York where I embarked once more, this time in a spirit of some desolation. I thought it unlikely I would ever see Harry again and knew that I would miss him dreadfully, as indeed I did. I also knew that I would never find another lover his equal.

But looking back over the years I find little trace of that great love affair in my heart. It is Doc I still miss; and whose photograph rests on my desk as I type. He lived to a great age and had the honour of carrying Mrs Breckenridge at a major event in her honour three years before she died in 1965. He died too, peacefully, a few years later. May their noble souls rest in peace.

CHAPTER TWENTY

LAHORE

1951 - 1953

"He sat in defiance of municipal orders astride the great gun Zam Zammah on her brick platform opposite the old Ajaib-Gher, the Wonder House, as the natives call the Lahore Museum".

Rudyard Kipling, 'Kim' Ch.1. Penguin 1994.

I have blocked out the memory of the voyage from New York and I can only recall the desolation of the parting from Harry and being in floods of tears in the cabin; and the woman in the other bunk, when I gave an incoherent explanation, saying, "you're lucky really, many people go through life without such an experience of love". As I write this I am conscious that my broken heart tends to heal with quite unseemly haste! But I have been devastated at the time.

Back in London I only had a few weeks to prepare for the job as a midwifery consultant with the World Health Organisation in Lahore so I had plenty to do to occupy my mind if not my heart.

It was 1951 and I was aged thirty two. It was four years since I had left India and the volunteer work with the Friends Service Council. The job in Kentucky was also with a voluntary society, and I had never earned much, or had such status as work with the United Nations offered. I remembered how in Calcutta, sitting in the Indian Coffee House, my friends and I had looked down on UN personnel with their expensive cars and privileged life styles, so far removed from the terrible poverty of the people they were there to serve. The friend with whom I stayed in London was shocked at the way I put aside any principles she thought I possessed, spending, with obvious pleasure, considerable sums of money advanced by the Organisation to buy evening dresses and other clothes thought suitable for a member of the United Nations. I was issued with a UN passport which would, at least in theory, afford protection if there was a national emergency, and added to my feeling of having gone up in the world, and being special. I would be earning a salary, probably the equivalent of what a minister was paid in Pakistan. I know that in some ways I am greedy and unscrupulous! But it is fair to say that in accepting the WHO job I was primarily motivated by the spirit of adventure and the chance once again to be on a pioneering venture designed to help poor mothers and their babies. But I did not have any qualms about accepting the perks and the status that went with the new job.

I arrived in Lahore in May 1951 at the hottest time of year. It was good to meet Dr Jean Orkney again whose work in Calcutta had been such an inspiration to me. The team in Lahore consisted of Dr Jean Orkney, our team leader, and three nurses who were from New Zealand and specialised in public health.

We were billeted at Nedous Hotel, an elaborate red stone Victorian building set back from the tree lined Mall, originally laid out by Colonel Napier in 1885. Further down the road were the magnificent Government buildings erected in the days of the Raj. They looked wonderful in the moonlight and I treasure the memory of biking home to the hotel from a midwifery case one night to see a large elephant wandering nonchalantly around Government House plucking hibiscus from the beautifully laid out surrounding gardens. I assumed he had escaped from the local zoo and that he was on a walkabout. I dismounted and wished him well, pulling down some more foliage for him before beating a rather hasty retreat.

Before starting work I had a couple of days to settle in and I went first to the museum immortalised in Rudyard Kipling's Kim, now the Lahore Museum and Technical Institute. The famous Zam Zammah Gun on which Kim perched has long since gone, but there is a terracotta plaque of the gun in its place, designed and made by Kipling's father, Director of the Archaeological School and Museum in the late 1880's. Rudyard Kipling himself was on the staff of the Lahore Civil and Military Gazette.

To be in Lahore was another fulfilment of my childhood dreams, the city said to have been founded by Alexander the Great of Macedonia, one of my heroes, in honour of his beloved horse Bucephalus, and home of Kim, my role model, clever, exploitative, adaptable, adventurous Kim, Little Friend to all the World.

Lahore, and indeed Pakistan, did not have the same emotional or intellectual fascination for me as India. Perhaps I share the nostalgia of my generation for undivided India. It takes more than the half a century since Independence to get that out of one's blood. But Lahore's history, and the association with Kipling, were enough to feed my romantic imagination and inner life. I think I have always needed this link with literature and history to balance the reality of working in the Third World – the heat, the inevitable illnesses, the frustrations inherent in trying to implement any programme, and the adaptation to a new culture.

West Pakistan, as it was then called, was a thousand miles away from East Pakistan which did not achieve its own nation state as Bangladesh until 1971. Lahore, known as the Pearl of the Punjab, was most affected by the violence and killing that followed partition in 1947, the year I left India. The partition of India resulted in the forced migration of twelve million people, appalling bloodshed and the total disruption of families and whole communities. The army, educational establishments and all vital services were left in chaos, and during my time in Lahore there was still great political unrest. The Prime Minister, Liaquat Ali Khan had been recently assassinated in Rawalpindi and military rule was imposed on more than one occasion. There were still thousands of unsettled refugees in the city.

The school of health studies was established near the Lady Dufferin Hospital with a maternal and child health clinic nearby in the shadow of the great Badshahi Mosque, built in the reign of Auranszeb. Its magnificent white domes pierced the skies in the early hours. Returning from midwifery cases I was awed by the dawn call to prayer from its tall minarets and the splendour of it all. This was my first contact with the Islamic world, as although I had met Muslims in Calcutta, the predominate culture there was Hindu and I had lived and worked from a Hindu household.

Our project entailed training community health workers and my energies were soon directed to the task I had been set – to teach theoretical and practical midwifery to the students who by then had received some grounding in community and public health. The students were all "Matric Pass" girls from high class families, recruited to qualify for work in the villages and small towns in the Punjab. All the girls, mostly aged about eighteen, spoke and wrote fluent English, and they all worked very hard and were a delight to teach.

The practical work centred on the maternal and child welfare clinic which was always crowded with pregnant women and infants and toddlers. Most women brought their mothers or mothers-in-law with them. Although we hoped to do preventative work the malnutrition and prevalence of serious illness in most of the patients had to take precedence.

The domiciliary side of the work was my special responsibility. I had a Muslim colleague, Miriam, known as my 'opposite number', who was expected to take over my role at the end of the contract. Together, we visited local homes in a defined area to build up a midwifery service. The work was much the same as the work I did in Calcutta in 1945.

Our area was mainly a refugee area, and the families lived in crowded rooms or makeshift structures on the narrow roads. There was little, if any, sanitation. It was the all too familiar setting of undernourished children, sick and overburdened mothers, and the inevitable diseases of poverty: tuberculosis, severe nutritional deficiency diseases and tropical illnesses. Why anyone thinks that such illnesses are prevented or cured only by vaccinations I can't think, when it is obvious that what is needed to prevent them are good sanitation and food. I doubted if the poor would inherit the earth, but at least I hoped that one day people would not starve to death. In those days I was not much given to ruminating about the social and political aspects of poverty so I got on with the job of giving such help as I could, teaching the students to give simple advice about nutrition and hygiene and the benefits of ante-natal care and a safe delivery.

Fortunately our first home deliveries went well, as this was important in building up trust in the community. I spent many hours with Miriam and our students sitting with the women of the patient's family in the stifling heat of the crowded room, drinking tea in little clay pots and smoking the hookah. After the baby was born, custom demanded that girl babies had their ears pierced, a task I usually delegated to Miriam, being of a nervous disposition myself, and afraid of not doing it properly.

One day in the clinic two women approached me. One, the senior wife, thin and exhausted with loose skin hanging in folds on her shrunken body, said she had had fourteen pregnancies, and how could she cope now the second wife, only sixteen years old, was herself pregnant. "How can we all be fed?" she lamented. "How can we stop having babies?" "We need medicine to stop babies coming". We tended the young wife as best we could, giving her the powdered milk and vitamin supplements provided by UNICEF, and consoling the older wife.

I discussed this case with Dr Orkney. It frequently happens in my life that momentous changes have followed the impact made on me by a significant isolated human incident. The older patient with her appalling burden of repeated pregnancies was a heart-breaking story, one of many no doubt, but this one, as it were, came to me to be dealt with. In the 1950's the Pill had not been invented.

Dr Orkney agreed that there could be no objection to incorporating birth control into our maternal care programme and gave me leave to "get on with it". It would have been wiser if she had first discussed it with government officials, WHO headquarters, and perhaps local Mullahs? If she had done so it is unlikely that any progress would have been made, but the pioneering enterprise was to get me personally into very serious difficulties later, well worth it in the long run, but changes in the status quo are not achieved without heads rolling. At the time I had no inkling that by promoting such an enterprise ahead of its time there would be political repercussions. I am not given to thinking far enough ahead about the results of my actions. Just as well perhaps. But to be fair to both Dr Orkney and myself, the local government in the Punjab was not the seat of power. That lay in Karachi which I was to learn later had strong views about birth control.

To make a start in this enterprise I called a meeting with the Lahore high born Begums; emancipated well-to-do women, the sort you often find are ready to promote some aspect of social reform, who have no reason to fear recriminations, and who enjoy Committee work and the status of public service. We planned to raise money, but were dependent on very small donations at first.

Fate intervened. I was sent as a delegate to a maternal and child welfare conference in Bombay. Sitting next to me in the hall was a quiet middle aged man, an American, who introduced himself as Dr Gamble, from the firm of Proctor and Gamble. This meant nothing to me, but he asked about my work and became very animated when I told him about the birth control clinic. He offered to help financially and told me about his birth control invention which consisted of inserting a small square of thin foam rubber, attached to a short cord, soaked in normal saline, up the vagina prior to intercourse. Saline, apparently, kills sperm and, according to Dr Gamble, was not only effective but cost next to nothing. It was convenient for poor women to use in their overcrowded homes where there was no hope of privacy or hygiene. To cut a long story short, miles of foam rubber arrived for us in Lahore, and so started the Family Planning Movement in the Punjab. I got on with my work, and birth control was included in the programme, backed up by a now flourishing voluntary committee of Lahore emancipated women. My next duty was to contact and liaise with other public health departments.

On one of these courtesy visits I met a Director whom I will call Hussein. We talked about our work, his desk littered with reports, the fan clanking overhead, the *peon* coming in and out with files, the telephone ringing constantly. The heat was unbearable. Hussein ordered iced lime juice. He explained that he was from Central India and had fled his home town with his mother and sisters during the communal riots. "They don't like me much here" he said "I don't take bribes. As perhaps you will agree that my office is not conducive to conversation" he said, "perhaps I could call on you at the hotel for tea?" As he was the most beautiful person I have ever seen in my life I raised no objection.

He came the same day. I made tea and watched entranced, as I did on many future occasions, his elegant hands holding the teapot, as he took on the customary male role of pouring tea: olive skinned, raven haired, and elegant, with the features of an Indian god. 'Coming to tea', usually on Thursday, became a routine in our lives and of such significance that, even now, my women friends who know of this romance, ask me from time to time "have you had anyone interesting to tea recently?"

I thought I was in love with Hussein but I suppose it was largely infatuation nurtured by propinquity and his astonishing beauty. He embodied all my romantic fantasies of India. Hussein's family had for generations been advisors to the Raj and to the Indian Princes and Hussein proudly carried on the tradition of service to the nation when he qualified as a doctor. He had few, if any, confidants, fearing intrigue in a country still highly politically unstable. Frequently I did not understand the content or implications of what he said, but long practice as a child of pretending to comprehend what was being said made it easy for me to look attentive and put in an occasional word of encouragement. Being afraid to look stupid does not worry me now that I have outgrown so many of my earlier fears and anxieties.

When he was not talking about his work and politics, Hussein taught me about Islam so that I began to have a basic understanding of the culture and religion. This was immensely helpful both for my work and in appreciating the beliefs and family lives of my students and patients.

The friendship between us grew as did our mutual attraction and we became lovers. Hussein was a virgin so that his first experience of sex took him quite by surprise. "Oh dear" he laughed, "now I shall have to get married". But for the next months, until the end of my two year contract, he seemed content with our weekly encounters, and they were indeed rapturous, although for me, without the full sexual satisfaction I had experienced with Harry who was a very considerate lover. But I would never have dreamed of explaining to Hussein about women's orgasms, so he had no reason to suppose that anything was lacking. I was so in love with him that our simple love-making was all I wanted. I shaved off my pubic hair to please him once I realised he found it offensive. Later in the villages I noticed in my work with Muslim women that they took great trouble to remove all body hair and rubbed the pubic area of their infant daughters with a piece of copper in the belief that this discouraged hair growth.

Hussein's work and mine often took us on tour and sometimes our visits coincided and we stayed in the same government building. At night I would wait longingly for the quiet sound of the door opening, for his hand to lift the mosquito net and to feel his lovely body.

Hussein talked about his responsibilities for his mother and two sisters. His father had been killed in the riots. They urged him to get married, as otherwise there would be no son to carry on the line. He told me later that he did not think it right to marry me as it would put an end to my career and he thought, probably correctly, that I would have found it very hard to adjust to living in a Muslim household. I went on living in my fool's paradise, as paradise it was, but I think Hussein's family was already looking for a suitable bride for him. He probably decided to leave things as they were until I finished my contract in Lahore.

Meanwhile, work continued. I enjoyed teaching midwifery as well as the practical side, and the students listened attentively, although I hoped my presentation improved after I read one girl's comment – "Miss Court's lectures are so interesting, I only wish I could hear them."

In the cooler weather we took the students to a remote village in the Punjab to give them experience of work in rural areas. The Punjab countryside is flat, but green and beautiful with cultivated land linked with the villages by mud roads and numerous canals draining from the five rivers of the Indus, creating lush fertility.

We taught the students to ride the bicycles donated by UNICEF and they found this hilarious. It crossed my mind that their parents were probably unaware of half that was going on in the training of their daughters to become community health workers.

I encouraged the students to respect local customs, and not to interfere with them unless they posed a health threat to the mother. There was no need, for example, to teach mothers how to breast feed as this was universal in the 1950's. We taught that it would be dangerous to impose the Western pattern of early weaning which could well lead to the infant developing malnutrition. There was a real danger in the 1950's of believing that we, so called experts from the West, knew what was best. Since then new threats to the uneducated poor have increased as unscrupulous drug and agrochemical industry and powdered milk manufacturers flooded the Third World with their products, posing one of the greatest health hazards, particularly to the children.

The students and I engaged in local research about customs and beliefs. We learnt how to place a special dried flower in a bowl of water when a woman was in labour so that when it opened the cervix would dilate too, and how to dispose of the placenta by burying it near to the hut entrance, and to hang the umbilical cord to dry from the ceiling to ensure the baby's survival. We also learnt the importance of getting home before dark for fear of meeting evil spirits who, with their feet turned backwards, could lead you to destruction. It was peaceful in the villages and in the evening, as we sat eating our chapattis and curry, the only sounds were of distant flutes and of women grinding spices and the thump of wood against stone separating the grain. It was a restful interlude from the clamour of traffic in Lahore and the stress of working in the heat of the clinic and overcrowded slum dwellings.

It was not peaceful when we returned to Lahore. There was martial law and rioting and Hussein was in hospital with appendicitis. I was very anxious about him and, recklessly disregarding danger in the streets, I drove to the hospital to see him and to take him fruit juice. He was making a good recovery and I drove back safely before the angry crowds stormed out of the Mosques. It was a Friday and no violence could occur before prayers.

At about the same time we experienced a slight earthquake. The sky darkened and the birds started flying round in agitation in the garden. We were all in one room having a team meeting. As the walls shook Dr Orkney shouted "get out." "After you" we said politely, as she shoved us out into the open.

There was very little damage other than a few more cracks in the decaying hotel structure and a few pieces of the pediment hurtling to the ground.

The hot season also brought a plague of locusts. The sky suddenly became as black as night as they swarmed over the city and soon the hotel was ankle deep in the poor creatures. We raced up to our rooms and closed the shutters and doors. I saved one little insect and fed him leaves and water. The rest were swept up and burnt and the leafless trees were the legacy of their visit.

The two years were drawing to an end. The project was thought to have been a success and I was busy writing a final report and having some difficulty in analysing the data. However, a mutual acquaintance gave my name to James, a professor from England visiting Lahore for a conference. I helped him settle into his hotel and accepted, without complaint, his agitated comments on my driving. I never really learnt to drive properly but I coped well enough in Lahore and Karachi, which demanded the ability to respond to the unexpected, particularly to camels who would lean angrily over the car bonnet, bells and blue necklaces rattling on the windscreen if I unintentionally denied them the right of way. James kindly came round a few times to help me assemble my report coherently. He made an impact on me as I had not met an academic before, and I was impressed by his clear thinking and grasp of facts. James was to have a significant influence on my life, not entirely benign.

It was time to leave Lahore. We were given a month's leave following which the team, minus alas Dr Orkney who had other plans, was to be transferred to Karachi to establish the same programme as we had in Lahore.

I parted from Hussein, who had made a good recovery from his operation, with a slight feeling of foreboding, but in the expectation that our relationship would continue, and, I hoped, lead to marriage. I assumed we would meet in Lahore as it would not have been difficult to fly there or take the night train. It is easy to disregard the small omens of pending disaster. The fact that Hussein made no commitment and said nothing about the future should have been enough to warn me of his intentions, which did not include marriage to me.

CHAPTER TWENTY ONE

KARACHI

1953 - 1955

Back in London on leave I talked obsessively to my women friends about Hussein in a manner more suitable to someone in her teens than a woman in her mid thirties. I built up a fantasy of marriage, complete with feasting, expensive gifts, shining wedding clothes, golden jewellery, and my loved one garlanded with marigolds riding a white horse surrounded by drummers. But even I realised that although it would be like this in a traditional ceremony, it might not be in accord with Hussein's status in society. I dreamed how I would live happily in his home, care for his mother, make close friends with his sisters, learn to cook the food he liked, bear his sons. I have sometimes regretted not having his child out of wedlock, but in the 1950's it would have been difficult, and in any case I left it too late, dreaming of a marriage which would not take place.

I wondered what I could take Hussein back as a gift, and eventually decided to buy him gold cuff links from Aspreys in Bond Street. I also bought a beautiful cobalt and blue bone china Aynsley tea-set from the Army and Navy Stores costing the then immense sum of ten pounds.

The month passed quickly and soon I was on the flight back to Pakistan with the tea-set in a canvas bag carefully wrapped in layers of tissue paper and happy to think I would soon see Hussein.

I stayed the first week in a hotel as the team members were expected to find their own accommodation. I went down to the courtyard after dark to feed the stray cats and found it full of camels bringing in their cartloads of fruit and vegetables. I attempted to give a banana to one of them, but he gave me a disdainful look, as only a camel can, and barred his yellow teeth at me. "Never mind" the camel driver said, "your intention was correct and you will acquire great merit with Allah the Merciful, who every night whispers into each creature's ear, has your master fed you today?" I learnt later that the reason camels look chronically offended, and have to be placated with coloured beads, tassels and other adornment to amuse them is because they were the last creature created by Allah who was concerned that no human being could exist in the desert without an animal to help them. So he created the camel with the remaining mud he had at hand, throwing the last handful at the poor creature so that the genitals are back to front. I do not know if this is in fact anatomically correct, or indeed if they are really disdainful when you get to know them.

Next morning at the hotel Gwen, one of the New Zealand nurses, came to see me bringing a bunch of flowers. I asked eagerly about Hussein. Had she any news of him? "Yes" she said "and there is no way I can break this to you gently really, but he asked me to tell you that he has agreed to an arranged marriage and that this will be quite soon in Karachi." "I don't actually think", she added, "that Hussein is very happy at the prospect, but I suppose he is doing what he believes is his duty in the family." I was inconsolable. Gwen stayed in the hotel for two nights and I clung to her in despair, weeping like a child.

Gwen found me a flat in St Mary's Road, in a leafy suburb. It consisted of one large sitting room with a couch and a bathroom and was reached by a spiral iron staircase on the first floor of a small block of apartments. The room was airy and light with wrought iron trellis at the windows. These could be shuttered at night, but in the day time allowed the chipmunks to come begging for the food they liked: raisins and nuts, which they ate like squirrels, chattering for more.

I settled in, hiring Abdullah, who came looking for a job clasping a pathetically torn reference. He was happy to take on all the work I required, simple cleaning, shopping and cooking. He explained that his family lived in a room near the apartments and I went to see them, the little family, his wife and two infants, smiling and welcoming in their tiny room. I noticed that Abdullah was toothless and he laughed and said "They all fell out when I was building the Burma Road in the war." When I had arranged for dental care for him, and dentures, he told me "I shall always remember you whenever I eat."

Karachi, then capital of West Pakistan, is near the coast. It seemed to me a town without character. Hot and dusty from the sands blowing in from the Sind desert, it practically never rained and the dry climate did not suit me. The city was crammed with refugees, living in appalling conditions. Our training school and the clinic were adjacent to a hospital and in a relatively settled refugee area. But by some oversight the building was not yet ready for us, so we set up the clinic as best we could while building continued around us. The builders were mainly young Sindhi peasant women, doing all the heavy work carrying bricks, their babies strapped to their backs and the older infants slung in little hammocks from the rafters. Men had laid the concrete floor using too much sand, so that in the early weeks Matron's bath water from the adjoining hospital seeped up, flooding us out. When this was remedied we began ante-natal work and I was delighted with the nurse appointed as my colleague, Hanifa Siddiqui, a Pathan from the North West Frontier. Like Bela, she became a life long friend and, also as with Bela, I later encouraged her to come to England for some academic training.

The clinic was on the outskirts of the refugee area which consisted of some overcrowded houses, and homes made of mud and straw sprawling on the roads, with corrugated tin roofs, or the roof of an old car or bus. At night you could hear the rats scrambling about on it. Cooking and washing were done outside the room on the road, and everywhere families were trying to scratch a living, children rolling *birees* and smoking them, others making baskets or clay pots or little packs of spices to chew.

The mothers who came to our clinic were, if anything, poorer than in Lahore. Many had tuberculosis and osteomalacea, a disease similar to rickets, which can lead to obstructed labour because the pelvis becomes deformed. Most were anaemic and some had very serious deficiency diseases such as pellagra, caused by a severe vitamin B deficiency. Tuberculosis was widespread, caused not only by malnutrition and overcrowding, but because the women were too poor to afford to have individual *burquas*, so they had to share them with other women in the family in order to observe the customary purdah. Our students wore the *burqua* when they went home at weekends, but their families agreed as one of the requirements of joining our school, that it would be in order if they simply wore a head scarf and veil during their time with us.

We worked hard, but my heart was not really in the job. Hussein came to my flat the night before his wedding. He looked withdrawn, remote, sadly preoccupied. I made him tea for the last time and gave him the cuff links. He said, in all seriousness I think, that I should have taught him about English literature, "Jane Austen and so on; my fiancée says I am uncultivated". He asked me how I thought he would feel shut up with a stranger on the long train journey back to Lahore. I felt no anger, only desolation. But now I am glad I did not teach him about Jane Austen or how to make love. I did not see him again for about 20 years when he came to London to settle his two daughters into university and to arrange for his son to be admitted to Eton. He looked like a prosperous, slightly overweight Italian film director. Sometimes I wonder as I bike around Cambridge if I shall one day see a ravishingly beautiful Indian in college, or at a graduation ceremony and think it could be one of his great-grandchildren.

In Karachi my reaction to the unresolved grief was quite manic. I threw myself into an amateur dramatic company based in the locality where I lived. It was an effort to found an interracial group, and there were a few professionals in the group to act as teachers and directors. They were welcoming and friendly and I enjoyed the warmth and company. I made friends with a young Armenian, Rashid Karapiet, who seemed very talented and for whom, as he explained, there was no future as an actor in Pakistan. He worked in radio but he wanted to be an actor. I offered to pay his fare to England and to introduce him to people who might advise him how to get into drama school. He achieved this but because, as he said "I am the wrong colour and too short" it took about thirty years before his talent was recognised and he had to retrain as a teacher to earn his living. But he never gave up, and I felt very proud for him when he started getting parts on television, in films and in West End plays.

I continued living quite recklessly in Karachi until the end of my contract, sleeping with a number of the UN men working on other projects and with so called visiting experts. I cared for none of them. But I made one real friend, a distinguished American social worker, Elmina Lucky, elderly, wise and sophisticated. She liked to visit me because she found it peaceful, a break from the hectic and controversial work she was immersed in, trying to develop a community project with local leaders. I was interested in all she told me as it was all new to me and she helped to lay the ground for my growing interest in social work.

I had no love life until Simon came. A round faced, large, solemn, seal point Siamese cat with the usual raucous Siamese voice, music to the ears of addicts. He lived with a couple in the next flat who also worked for one of the UN agencies. They had inherited Simon from some other Americans who had returned to the States. He was about seven years old, and must have had at least four "owners". The present couple didn't really appreciate him, claiming that his face was too round for a "proper pedigree" Siamese, but they felt responsible for him. As they were going on a month's leave, they wondered if I would look after him during their absence. I was glad of an opportunity to do them a favour. The poor things had been subjected to harassment from the noisy gatherings in my flat, entertaining the theatre group and holding rehearsals, accompanied at times by the drums and flutes of "noises off" as Roman armies approached. We were very inconsiderate, but I disliked their disapproval of the company I kept and their racist comments – "We don't know why you want to mix with local people so much…"

Simon sat on the dining room table, gave himself a wash, and accepted Abdullah's offering of a little steamed fish in white sauce. I raised Abdullah's wages as he now had another person to care for. I was glad to have a pet in the house, but the relationship between us took time to mature as I had never lived with a Siamese before, and indeed I had not had a cat since I had dear Emma put to sleep in 1945, a decade before. But it was not long before we grew to love each other, and by the third week I was really dreading the return of his "owners". He was such a self contained cat person, happy to be alone with me, to be waited on and brushed by Abdullah when I was at work, and in the evenings and at weekends to grace my parties, sitting in the middle of the circle, accepting the homage due to him or chasing a stray olive or crisp to amuse us, or interrupting our rehearsals with an occasional howl of disapproval or acclaim. Sometimes he was our severest critic, but at other times he curled up happily and sang his appreciation.

The neighbours returned and came round to claim him. He did not want to be claimed but there was nothing I could say. Pets, after all, are little more than slaves with no real control over their lives.

But Simon did his best to return to me, sitting at the barred window so that every time I passed along the outside corridor on my way to work he would yowl his head off, egged on unceremoniously by me putting my hand through the bars and saying "keep it up darling", fondling his ears the way he liked. Soon neighbours were complaining about the noise he made and his owners complained that he had forgotten how to use the litter tray. I said how sorry I was, and that perhaps I had spoilt him with too much attention. They agreed and said "You'd better have him back then, and when we get back to America we will get ourselves a proper pedigree." And so Simon returned, sitting on the table as he did when he first came, giving himself a thorough wash as if to say "that's that then" and welcomed Abdullah who came racing up the spiral staircase with a hastily prepared offering of shelled prawns.

My home life settled and I felt more able to concentrate on work. But unknown to me storm clouds were gathering as rumours about my involvement in family planning reached the ears of the Ministry of Health in Karachi. We did not include birth control in the Karachi programme but various birth control specialists contacted me from abroad on their way to Lahore where apparently the movement was gaining great momentum. As Dr Orkney wrote in her assessment "Joan Court is a suitable candidate for promotion, but needs to watch that her enthusiasms do not run away with her."

Our team leader called me to her office, looking very troubled and embarrassed. She said she had received a very serious complaint from WHO Regional Headquarters in Alexandria about my unauthorised work promoting family planning in Lahore. The complaint came from the Ministry of Health in Karachi. It was, therefore, proposed that I should be transferred as soon as practical to another project in Africa. I do not know, and it never occurred to me to ask, if Dr Jean Orkney was contacted for an explanation.

I was told that I should seek an appointment with Colonel Jaffa, the Minister of Health, as soon as possible. Our team leader went on kindly to say that she had no criticism of my work and that she would be giving me an excellent appraisal.

The interview with Colonel Jaffa was less alarming than I had expected. Although by then I was feeling slightly annoyed at being made a scapegoat for a campaign which I had initiated, but about which the 'powers that be' had raised no objection at the time, this was accompanied by an ominous feeling of guilt. It has often struck me that, in spite of having pioneered a number of enterprises throughout my life, I remain at heart quite frightened of what I achieve or try to achieve. This is not the more common neurotic fear of failure but, I suppose, fear of success as if, as a psychiatrist once remarked "you think you are getting away with it."

Colonel Jaffa did not ask me to sit down but gave a sigh and looked up from his mountain of files. "You should know perfectly well, Joan, that we need sons for our Army if we are to survive as a Nation." It had not occurred to me that this would be the main reason why birth control would be opposed. I expected, if anything, that there might be objections from traditional Muslims. I told him that I was only concerned for the health of women and children, and that I would like to stay on in Pakistan and to finish my contract. Colonel Jaffa looked at me briefly and said sternly "All right, go back to work and don't let me hear any more about this nonsense."

I was very shaken by this experience and more so when later that week a senior WHO nurse, not involved in our programme but with overall responsibility for nursing programmes in Pakistan, remarked, probably annoyed that I had not been removed as she disliked me intensely, "the trouble with you, Joan Court, is that you are more interested in social work than you are in nursing, and I can't imagine why your name is always in the WHO nursing newsletters. "Because I write vivid reports" I did not reply as I would now, I hope, although I still find it difficult to cope with the envy and jealousy I frequently arouse. I think her comment about my interest in social work was because of my close relationship with Elmina Lucke and my interest in her community welfare programme. There was compartmentalisation between agencies, and professional jealousy. I, on the other hand, like to forge links between different "tribes" who can work together. This sometimes naïve approach can lead to disaster, as it once nearly did in Calcutta when at the height of the riots I called a meeting of Hindu and Muslim leaders in the area with a view to returning peace in our district. Bela, quite rightly, was terrified as, although the meeting began well, knives were soon drawn and we had to beat a hasty retreat.

I am of the view that one learns less from experience than is commonly believed and that it is more likely that one repeats the same errors of judgement and action, perhaps modified if one is as lucky as I have been in having wise mentors. Jung wrote that it does no harm to give advice as no one takes it. This is not quite true in my case as I have been fortunate in meeting wise people at different stages of my life, but I remain impetuous and often angry and exasperated at the slowness of change in the causes I promote. These have changed as society catches up with my vision: family planning is now fully accepted in Pakistan and I have moved on to other frontiers. As Dr Orkney wrote – "Joan Court always knows what she wants to do and why", but it is the boost of encouragement from people I respect and love which has so often enabled me to carry forward a plan.

The senior nurse was far from encouraging and I began to feel an outcast, a common feeling you get when you are fired, likely to be fired, made redundant, suffer a bereavement or have a fatal illness. But what she said about my overriding interest in social welfare registered. I knew that if I stayed on in WHO I would end in being promoted to a senior post, probably in administration. Did I want this? I had only a vague understanding of social work but I had noticed from the time I was a health visitor in London that social workers were more creative and thoughtful, and less dogmatic and authoritarian than doctors and nurses who usually assumed that they knew what was best for people. Perhaps it was time I made a change of direction? And I still nurtured the dream of higher education, the 'schooling' I had missed out on as a child.

I talked about this with James, the visiting academic I had met briefly in Lahore who was now also in Karachi on a planning mission. He was not keen on me leaving nursing, projecting on me, I think, some Florence Nightingale image. He suggested we discuss it further and asked me to accompany him to the North West Frontier to help him understand what the women in that area wanted for themselves. They, not surprisingly, said "what we want is health care for our families, especially for our children." James thought I would be the ideal person to pioneer such a project. I pointed out that I had no intention of being a martyr in such a dangerous area. He commented "but someone has to be".

Our trip from Rawalpindi and Peshawar to the North West Frontier is not something I would have missed. Shades of Kipling and Kim again, and what was known throughout the days of the Raj as the Great Game: the diplomatic machinations and intrigue aimed at keeping the neighbouring, warring Afghan tribes at bay, the Russians from invading, and local tribesmen from engaging in more warfare and assassinations than strictly necessary. We travelled north, accompanied on the Front by an armed escort through to Waziristan, staying in fortified garrison towns, eating our meals in the officers' mess, soberly watched by photos of noble Chitral scouts that decorated every wall.

We stayed at a school on the way back and a teacher said to James, referring to me, "What is she to you ?" This was not meant rudely but just as a polite enquiry about our relationship. James made some suitable reply but I felt slightly amused as by then I had seduced him, partly I think from irritation at his inept and irritating attempts to kiss me. But my analyst commented in years to come "I think you often slept with men for the conversation." There is some truth in this. James was the most enthralling companion and story teller and a brilliant public speaker. Once he was on his feet at any meeting, you could relax knowing that he would have a full grasp of the material, present it with wit and intelligence, and that no one, ever, could fall asleep as long as he was on his feet. What I brought to him, I think, apart from erotic joys to which he was unaccustomed, was contact with an unconventional person with a wild and independent streak, unlike the academics and the serious minded students he normally encountered. He seemed quite fascinated with my life and I confided to him about my background. In lay terms I suppose he was a father figure, and the relationship became a major influence in my life. He was certainly helpful once he accepted that I was serious in my intention to change careers, but he did not really approve of older people getting into higher education, regarding them as perpetual students. I don't know what he would think now of the concept of education continuing throughout life, and the high proportion of mature students in universities.

I wondered about training at the LSE but James thought it would be better if I went to a redbrick university away from the noise and distractions of London. The university he favoured was the one where he occasionally taught. I believe he meant well, and one can't say worse than this. In the event I applied to both universities and was accepted by both. The redbrick place asked me to write an extended essay about my present work and what I hoped to gain from training in social work. The LSE set a formal examination. I feared the questions would be about my understanding of politics and/or economics. Fortunately this was not the case, but they included such gems as "Describe the changing status of masters and servants in the 20th Century." Shades of Compton Burnett's novels, and indeed of my own experiences at Parsonage Farm. Another: "What do you think is the role of students in modern Britain?" and "What is your view about the influence of horror comics on children?" I must have had a wonderful time writing these essays as I remember them so clearly. I accepted the offer from the provincial university believing that James knew best, and also glad that I would have his support.

The end of the Karachi contract posed a serious dilemma. What to do about darling Simon? It would have been possible to find a new home for him, but as Rashid, my Armenian actor friend said so wisely, "What sort of fate is that for him, always as it were on short term contracts, never with a settled home. It's a risk taking him but worse to leave him here." So we made preparations for his journey. The theatre people made him a comfortable travelling box and I booked his passage and filled in the necessary papers. The last weeks were spent in finding a new job for Abdullah and making sure he was happily settled, filing reports and going to parties, including one, not in our honour, but the Government reception for King Hussein of Jordan, a very grand affair. I had my usual bag at my feet in which to put tit bits for Simon, and the Ambassador, sitting next to me, looked mildly surprised as several chicken legs vanished from my plate – "They're for my cat" I said "who was unable to attend." "Ah", he said politely "what a good thing it isn't curried chicken", forking some chicken liver over to my plate.

In thinking of Simon's future I did not envisage the horrors of quarantine, but there it was and we boarded the plane, Simon mildly sedated. We travelled first class and Simon was not in the hold, thank goodness, but in his box in the luggage rack near the cockpit. A kindly steward became worried that under sedation he might suffocate and allowed him to finish the flight on my lap where he slept peacefully to the amazement of other passengers who came to admire him. Flying over London I looked out and saw it was snowing. This was in May 1955. My heart sank and soon the terrible moment came when I had to hand him over to the RSPCA Inspector who was responsible for keeping him overnight and then taking him to the quarantine kennels. I asked to stay and to go with him on the journey but this was out of the question.

No wonder I fought, before it became accepted practice, for parents to be allowed to stay with their children in hospital and for husbands to be allowed to keep their wives company when they are in labour. It is dreadful to have to part from loved ones when they are in crisis, suffering and lonely and needing you there.

Simon 1960

CHAPTER TWENTY TWO
TRANSITION
1955 - 1956

Simon's time in quarantine from May to October coincided with the months I had to fill in before going to university. I stayed in London and for the first few months I only visited Simon two or three times a week as he seemed to be coping. But I knew that other cats were ill, and I lived in perpetual dread that he would get cat 'flu which was very virulent in those days. In Karachi he sometimes had colds and sore throats, and I would give him shots of antibiotics, but he would have no resistance to the infections he would encounter in a strange environment and there was the added risk of being with other cats. The staff in the kennels were caring but without barrier nursing of the sick cats I feared cross infection. Each cat had his or her own feeding bowl but only one broom was used to sweep out all the cubicles.

Whilst things went well I wondered about taking a temporary nursing job but I decided instead that after four years in the elevated heights of semi-diplomatic life it would be a good thing if I did an ordinary job to bring me back down to earth as it were. I doubt if this was really necessary, as my ability to adapt to changed circumstances borders on the pathological, but the job I chose was as a waitress in a restaurant in central London. I was good at carrying trays – not for nothing had I carried seven bed pans down the long wards of St Thomas's Hospital. The job was quite a revelation. The workers' conditions were abysmal, the pay unregulated by trade unions, and if there were health and safety regulations they were not apparent. The kitchen floor in the basement was filthy with grease spills. I decided that I would never eat in such a restaurant again, but stick as far as possible to workmen's cafes when I wanted to snack, where you could usually see what was going on in the kitchen. Down in the basement the chef would stir a huge vat of jelly with his hands, up to the shoulder with his hairy arms, threshing around until it was the right consistency to be spooned out delicately into little glass bowls.

We were not supposed to take individual tips but I was shown how to quickly put any offerings we were given into the heel of my shoe. I did not stay long in the job as a message from the quarantine kennels informed me that Simon was unwell. He had a slight temperature - he might be incubating 'flu. Filled with foreboding I collected warm shawls, a hot water bottle, Brand's Essence and books to read, and started on the first of the daily journeys to nurse my beloved cat. Wrapped up together on the concrete floor I gave him little drops of fluid from a pipette and licks of Brand's Essence on my fingers. He was very ill but the vet was hopeful because she saw that he had the will to live. I read Hugh Walpole and Proust and stayed with him until dark. Visitors were not allowed to stay at night but I was back again first thing in the morning. I remember those days as winter. There could be no Spring as long as Simon was ill.

Simon began to get better and I was able to tempt him with snippets of braised kipper. His blocked nose and sinus meant he did not really fancy anything else, although once he started eating I knew he was over the worst. All the other Siamese cats in the kennels died in the epidemic, but brave Simon made a full recovery apart from mild chronic sinusitis which meant he continued to sneeze over everything and everybody for the rest of his life. It was good to hear him purring again and at last the glorious day came when I could take him home to purr in bed with me. Nowadays I have many friends in prison for crimes against the State such as rescuing beagle dogs from laboratories and breeding centres, and setting fire to trucks used for conveying live animals for export, or for conspiracy to liberate animals. I know that for many the separation from their pets is one of the worst things to bear, and, unfortunately, visiting rights in prison do not extend to animals, as they do increasingly in hospitals and residential homes.

James found me a comfortable room in a shared house near the University and Simon and I settled in. There was a small walled garden with a bomb site beyond where Simon soon learnt to catch the pigeons and terrorise other cats who, until then, thought they had exclusive territorial rights. It was Simon's first taste of freedom and he took to it as to the manner born. James came to see me before term began and he decided to show me the references he had written about me to both Universities. "Joan is a gifted young woman with a talent for getting on with people from all walks of life and all ages. In spite of missing out on formal education (her parents were mentally ill, her mother a chronic alcoholic and her father suffered from depression leading to suicide) she has had a distinguished nursing career, and she deserves credit for overcoming a delinquent background." He went on to write about my intelligence and his confidence that I would benefit from the course and the contribution my maturity would make to the student body.

I was devastated by James's betrayal of confidence as I had talked to him about my family and life experiences without any thought that he would share this knowledge with anyone, let alone in references. I felt labelled and stigmatised as, until then, I had never considered my parents to be mentally ill, but I remembered my grandparents saying that Peter and I had "bad blood" when I was showing signs of being an incipient radical in becoming a vegetarian and a pacifist.

I was afraid that the knowledge of my family background would influence how my tutors and supervisors would see me and judge my work. The worst blow to self esteem was his comment about my so called delinquent background. To be fair to James he was not referring to my time as a child shoplifter, but to my generally chaotic and neglected home life. Many years later when I talked about all this with my analyst, she said "rubbish, it was not delinquent, but the back-cloth for adult depression."

I think James acted in good faith, as at that time intending applicants for social work training were questioned about their family background (with the intention of rejecting those most likely to project unresolved conflicts on their clients), but unintentionally he broke through the protective defences I had, until then, maintained with some success. Repression can serve to maintain sanity and it doesn't do to take the lid off in such an insensitive manner. I had no way of dealing with the turmoil this engendered other than to turn to James for comfort. This cast rather a shadow on our continuing affair and contributed to a long period of anxiety and depression.

There were other factors which made the transition from nursing to social work difficult. In those days nurses and midwives were deeply appreciated and valued and always welcomed in the homes of their patients. Social workers, with their more complex tasks, rarely have the same welcome, even less nowadays when they have to be agents of social control in implementing the mental health and child care laws. I was not given to introspection then, and although I was always keenly aware of the suffering of my patients, and empathetic towards them, I had never had to think deeply about the complexity of social and personal influences that led to deprivation. I had always had an uncritical and hungry attitude to knowledge, believing what I was taught without question. In my day, nurses were taught what to do and were expected, as in the army, to be disciplined and efficient; not attributes to be sneered at, but of limited value in social work. I carried into my new career very little understanding of theory and concepts, or of what are called broader issues. In the first term I frequently did not understand what was being taught, but I dutifully took notes, hoping that light would dawn. James lectured in social policy and as I was interested in social reform and reformers and in the thinking behind the birth of the welfare state, this course was of great interest to me. Unfortunately, I was incapable then of taking part in seminar discussions. I did not have the intellectual tools or the confidence to speak, but I wrote perceptive and interesting essays so my tutors must have realised that I was capable of learning. I had, by then, made friends with a young girl half my age, but who, even at the age of eighteen, had a gentle and discerning wisdom. She too was experiencing emotional conflicts with a family rift caused by the rigid power of the sect to which she belonged, the Plymouth Brethren. We supported each other for the next two years and when I was feeling suicidal Suzanne would remind me "the key is under the flower pot by the front door step, you know you can come round any time." We shared all our thoughts and feelings then, and we continue to do so.

We had an exciting time on the course too, although it was in many ways fragmented and unsuitable for social work students. We shared classes with history and philosophy undergraduates, taught in a way which could be of little benefit to us, but both Suzanne and I were entranced by philosophy, our first exposure to Platonic theory. We both did well in the end of term exams, but it was just as well that we only had a brief encounter with philosophy as I would have soon have been lost in the more abstract theories. It would have been of more value to me and to all aspiring social workers if we had read ethics – it might have helped me to sort out my values – but I could never have grasped logic. Chaos theory would have been more my scene.

I did well in psychology and so began an interest in psycho-dynamic theories of human behaviour, but I barely passed the tests in local government administration and politics, the former because it was so boring and the latter because it involved wider issues beyond my comprehension and range of interests.

Suzanne and I had practical placements in the vacation and did well in them, supervised as we were by a robust and life-affirming case worker whom we both liked and respected. But I clung to James in the continuing depression as if he was a lifebelt rather than driftwood. I can see why I grew so dependent on him. He was eminent, brilliant and intelligent, a church elder, established in the world and highly respected in all the circles he moved in. I remember he was asked to lecture on modern sexual attitudes to an international gathering of the YWCA. He was a little apologetic to me when he rehearsed his paper, in which he argued that single women should value chastity, as if he wondered if I would think he was hypocritical.

Although I was doing well academically and in practical work, it was obvious to my tutor that my level of anxiety was a matter for concern. At home I was finding it difficult to make small decisions, hesitating for hours on whether to buy Carr's or Jacob's water biscuits when I had guests for supper, and weeping into the frying pan (always a bad sign) sleeping badly and dragging myself to lectures, saving energy to cope with academic demands.

I tried, too, to keep in touch with my friends in Asia, and both Bela and Hanifa, my good colleagues from Calcutta and Karachi, came to study in the UK. I also saw a great deal of Rashid, who was doing very well in drama school. But, although there was this continuity, I suspected that my life as a pioneer in the developing world was at an end. From time to time, over the years, I applied for exotic jobs in Africa, the Caribbean and the Gilbert and Ellis Islands, but I did not pursue them, or they did not pursue me. I no longer had the practical skills needed, and although I later became academically qualified to teach social work, other patterns of work emerged which changed my career.

My tutor, noting my pallor and increasing withdrawal, realised that I might have a breakdown if I did not have professional help and suggested I go for a weekend or two to Withymead, a psycho-therapeutic Jungian centre in Somerset where distraught students were referred. It was run by a doyenne of Jungian psychology, Irene Champernowne, and combined psychotherapy with the arts. I was not interested in dancing or painting, but found the whole ambience of the place healing, and Irene Champernowne helpful and perceptive. I was able to talk to her about my dilemmas in the relationship with James, and about his reference. She put this in proportion but she was concerned that the new career I had chosen was especially hazardous for someone with my background, exposed as I would continue to be to my clients' problems and their depression. She did not think I would recover from my present anxious and depressed state without a long term analysis, but felt that the time was not right for such a commitment. It would be better postponed, she thought, until I was in a settled job, as being a student could lead to regression which is potentially dangerous to vulnerable individuals, and analysis could precipitate a depressive breakdown. So I continued to go to Withymead for the occasional weekend until the two years of study were completed.

Suzanne and I both obtained our Testamur in Social Work. She went straight into a job locally, snapped up by our nice practical work supervisor, who knew a good thing when she saw it, and recognised that Suzanne was a born case worker. I had been talking to graduate students who encouraged me to apply for a degree, which they thought I should have done in the first place. Always an élitist, and having had a glimpse of the golden city, I asked James and my tutor for references to St Anne's in Oxford. No nonsense about family background now! Oxbridge is only interested in the candidate's intellectual calibre. It is just as well that I was turned down by St Anne's, but to me it was a glimpse of the promised land to be filed away for the future. I was not accepted at St Anne's because I had no foreign language and the admissions tutor thought I might find it difficult to reach an acceptable level of French in the first term as the curriculum required. Not difficult, but impossible actually, as would have been the course I'd planned in Politics, Economics and Philosophy. I was advised to try Leeds University which did not require a second language, but I thought Leeds would be a come-down, and elected instead to apply to the London School of Economics for the course leading to the qualification of psychiatric social work. In those days it was usual for social work aspirants to do a basic course, such as I had completed, and to go on to professional training in medical social work to become what was then called a Lady Almoner, or in mental health to specialise in psychiatry.

Child Care was at that time undeveloped, and generic social work, which later swept the field, was not on the horizon. The interview at the LSE went well. I made up a fictionalised account of my childhood, with just enough conflict in it to be credible and to show I had insight into family dynamics. I knew, or hoped, that James's reference would be filed away in the undergraduate department and would never appear in the mental health certificate cabinets, and this proved to be so.

CHAPTER TWENTY THREE

LONDON SCHOOL OF ECONOMICS

1957 - 1959

From 1957 I was in London, a student at the LSE in Houghton Street, near the Royal Courts of Justice where I was to spend much time as a child care specialist in the distant future. But in 1957 I was still an inhibited anxious student, unable sadly to take any advantage of the LSE's radical political teaching.

The mental health course, unlike the fragmented social work department I had just left, was focused, intellectually stimulating and well taught. My tutor was urbane and at our first meeting set me an essay: 'Outline the main differences between a neurosis and a psychosis.' I was amazed to be asked to write on a subject about which I knew virtually nothing. I thought that one went to lectures before having one's knowledge tested, but of course, I did not let on, and got on with my first piece of research.

As usual, my written work was excellent, but I managed to get through every seminar without saying a word. I was petrified, literally, of having to say anything in public. I attempted to deal with this handicap by enrolling in a friendly course in public speaking, but when, in the second session, we were asked to prepare a five minute presentation on how to plant a window box, I got as far as the word 'geranium' and then fled the room in panic and tears. It is still a miracle to me that I found my voice in the end. This happened much later in America when I noted that if students did not participate in class discussion they were given lower grades. Many factors may lie behind such a phobia and it is of little concern if life does not require you to overcome it. In my case I think the inhibition began when I discovered that I was invisible to my mother if I kept quiet and did not intrude on her alcoholic fury and so I would be less likely to be hit. But behind the fear of being heard lies the wish to be heard, and nowadays the latter is for me uppermost.

My home life in London at that time was unstressful. Simon and I shared a maisonette with Hetty, a Quaker who loved cats, and Simon adapted contentedly to being a house cat for the next two years as we did not have a garden. On the way back from college I would raid the immaculate garden of a nearby block of flats for the delicious blades of green grass growing at the edges that he needed for his digestion and to wind round fur balls.

The mental health course included two periods of clinical experience, four months in a mental hospital and an equal period in a child guidance clinic. My first placement was in the Maudsley Hospital known for its enlightened care of the mentally ill, but also, alas, as I discovered forty years later, for its terrible and cruel research using primates and cats. But I was then quite ignorant of this and I would not have known what to do with the information then even had I been informed of it.

My tutor at the hospital was Edgar Miles, a very experienced psychiatric social worker, unthreatening but astute and enabling in our supervision sessions. He made some comment about my anxiety which I did not find disturbing and told me "you underestimate your insights and abilities." I replied responsively "A lot of people have told me that." "Now I'm telling you" he said, and his authority had the same effect on me as Sister Mary's remark in the convent school "We expect great things of you one day Joan", a much needed ego boost.

I liked working with mentally ill adults. In those days social workers were taught case work and we kept process notes recording, as far as we could, what had been said in the interview and our observations. I did not find this threatening as I liked reflecting on the patient's story and working on an assessment of what was happening in the patient's life to cause the illness. As a nurse I was always aware that symptoms might have a physical cause , although at that time there was less awareness than there is now of the body/ mind link.

My own depression did not lift, although I do not think that any of my patients were aware of it. My persona and attentive listening and my genuine concern were, I knew, reassuring and professional. But outside clinical sessions I, no doubt, looked anxious and preoccupied, as the canteen lady once remarked when I went to buy matches, "I'm sorry dear, we can't sell matches to patients, ask one of the staff for a light." I thanked her politely.

When this placement was completed, Edgar Miles showed me his assessment, puffing away on one of his perpetual cigarettes. He wrote very positively of my work, but added that "Joan's evident anxiety should be carefully watched."

I moved on to my child guidance placement in a well established, historic centre in Osnaburgh Street. There, once again, I was blessed with a wise older supervisor, Hilda Horder, who had the endearing habit of talking kindly to her files as she came up the stairs. She welcomed me, showed me where to make coffee, and then giving me a few files said "you can read through these if you like, sit by the fire", and left me for about a week undisturbed. This reminds me of the method I use with frightened cats who come to live with me nowadays. They come out from under the bed eventually, but they are tamed by warmth, food and the absence of any disturbance. It is, of course, possible that Hilda Horder simply forgot I was there, but I think not. Passing my chair one morning she said "Would you like to come up to my room now to talk over one of those cases you've been reading, so we can decide which one you would like to start on?", and so began a relationship which formed the basis of my professional growth as a social worker. At the end of the placement I sent Hilda Horder flowers and asked her if she would come to the theatre with me. She accepted and became one of the wise women who have guided my life including Sister Mary, the Reverend Mother in Cape Town, "Home Sister" in St Thomas' Hospital, Elmina Lucke and many others. They may be archetypes but they are also women I have loved and respected, almost as gurus, but without the absolute spiritual authority implied in such relationships.

During my time at the centre, I attended numerous case conferences and because I objected to patients ever being discussed in a way other than with total respect, I noted the quiet understatements and tender way that one child psychiatrist presented her cases. It is tempting to make the occasional disparaging or flippant remark about clients and patients, and most of us are guilty of this, but Dr Margaret Collins was not. I thought at the time, "if ever I want an analyst I'd like to have her – a pity she doesn't deal with adults" assuming she only dealt with children.

Before I completed the mental health course, Edgar Miles suggested I apply for a vacant post in the Walthamstow Child Guidance Clinic as, although this would mean a lot of travelling (I was living in Kilburn), he wanted me to have the benefit of working in a first class clinic setting which would help to consolidate my training and develop my interest in psychodynamic theory. I was accepted for the post and started work at once.

At about that time, although I was still meeting James for illicit weekends staying usually at the Great Western Railway Hotel in Paddington, or at a more posh one off Piccadilly, I was beginning to find the deception and secrecy a burden. I liked his wife and felt uneasy, an uneasiness not shared by James. "If anything", he commented, "you have improved the quality of our marriage, and it would simply never occur to her that you and I were other than dear friends." I do know that our relationship enriched his life, I was dear to him, as he was to me, and the note of bitterness which creeps into my account of those times is only a partial and perhaps residual overflow from a time of my life which was, on all counts, very unsettled.

Whatever the motivation I decided to drift out of his life and I think he believed it was for moral reasons which he felt bound to respect. It is more likely that I was too depressed to cope with any more emotional demands.

But I was becoming more exhausted and depressed and matters came to a head one winter morning. I was in the train, in a closed carriage on my own, without a corridor. Suddenly I felt a terrible murderous presence, evil and overpowering. No visible person was there but the projection of this overpowering presence was intent on making me throw myself out of the carriage. The hatred was palpable, as it was when I was a child and mother threatened to kill me and skin me alive (like the poor dogs and cats in the Far East?). The terror and the evil force battled for my life and I slid to the floor and crouched, with my head between my knees, knowing that if I stood up I would have flung myself from the train. At Walthamstow, I left the train, the evil projection vanished from my mind, but I was shaken by what I knew to be a psychotic episode that might recur. I realised that the original trauma stemmed from the days when I would race up to Pinner Station, sometimes alone, sometimes with Peter, and hide in the station master's office until the train to Rickmansworth came in. We would hear mother shouting and screaming in drunken fury as our protector denied having seen us.

I arrived a little late at the clinic, saw my first clients, and that night went home by bus. I would never feel safe again in a closed railway compartment. I knew then that I must take steps to preserve my sanity, so that night I telephoned Irene Champernowne in Withymead and asked her if she could refer me to an analyst. She said she would discuss this with her colleagues and write to me soon. She did so within the week, recommending Dr Margaret Collins, the psychiatrist whom I had watched in the child guidance clinic. I was very happy to learn that she saw adults in her private practice. I telephoned her and made my first appointment. I sometimes wonder who my Guardian Angel is, and why my extraordinary life manages to fall into such beautiful patterns, and particularly the way a significant person appears at every crossroad in my life. Serendipity? But they do not feel like chance encounters.

CHAPTER TWENTY FOUR

PSYCHOANALYSIS

1959 - 1963

For the next four years, analytical sessions with Dr Margaret Collins were central to my life and no doubt saved it. There are many critics of psycho-analysis and psychotherapy but I doubt the validity of much so called objective research, particularly when it is directed towards observing and explaining the inexplicable. What helps people in mental distress is far from clear and I tend to have more faith in dolphin therapy than in drugs, though they too can be life-saving if all else fails.

I remember Dr Donald Winnicott, the original and deeply loved paediatrician and analyst, remarking to my NSPCC team in 1969 when we were thinking of ways we could help abusive parents, "you know it doesn't really matter what you say to clients, you can say 'cabbages, cabbages, cabbages', and it will be felt as comforting and reassuring if you are in tune with their need." The therapeutic alliance formed between the healer and the client/patient is quite mysterious. John, a physicist boyfriend who winds his way in and out of my life, burdened with astronomical intelligence, once remarked "If you can believe in the quantum theory, you have to believe in God", and I continue to be attracted by the inexplicable. I did not know what I expected from analysis but I felt safe and contained as I sat in M.C.'s quiet room.

She was a slightly built, grey haired woman, an army officer's daughter, in her fifties, undramatic and as unlike my vivacious, erratic, distraught mother as it was possible to imagine. She had a remote tenderness, but she was not superficially warm or reassuring, and her quiet manner disguised a strength I learnt to value in the turbulent years ahead. She used no psychological jargon in the rare interpretations she made in relation to what was happening in our sessions, and I consequently, perhaps, have an arrogant contempt for much of what passes as 'counselling' nowadays, with its pseudo-analytical jargon.

In the first hour she told me that she thought I should come three times a week from 7 to 8 pm. I knew that the analytical hour was fifty five minutes, to allow a short break between patients and to ensure we did not meet on the doorstep. Not that meeting other patients seems to trouble people in analysis, engrossed as they are in their own intense relationship with the analyst as an infant is with its mother.

She asked me a few questions about my background and why I had come for treatment. I told her that I wanted a conducted tour of my childhood and not to go mad, as had been happening on my own. And I then retreated into silence, a silence which was to continue for many weeks ahead. This was followed by torrential tears, for which I apologised profusely. "Why, are not you allowed to weep?" M.C. asked.

In analysis you leave your persona aside, so in my case the self confident, resourceful and sometimes amusing impression I gave to the world had no place in the consulting room where we sat, armchairs strategically placed so that we were not too far apart or too close. Although, unlike in classical Freudian analysis, M.C., a Jungian, did not present herself as a blank screen, she was sufficiently detached and neutral, sometimes maddeningly so, to allow me to project my feelings onto her, particularly in relation to buried feelings about mother, and later, my father.

I think it was Freud who wrote that it was the duty of the analyst to stay alive and to be dependable. M.C. kept strictly to appointments and gave warning about times when she would be on holiday. I knew from the first day, for instance, that she would not be available in August or on public holidays, and when she had to go into hospital for a minor operation I had six months warning. I found out how much this dependability meant for me when, on one occasion, the first and only one in all the years we worked together, she was ten minutes late. No-one answered the door. I waited patiently on the step, my head in a book, knowing that she had met with an accident on her way from the clinic, shades of my mother lost in Ruislip woods, or weaving her way back to Pinner, singing to herself, oblivious of the traffic. When M.C. arrived she was not for a moment taken in by my apparent composure, noting my shaking hands as I lit a cigarette, turning up the gas fire, switching on the lamps and shutting out the darkness as she drew the curtains.

I both dreaded and longed for the sessions, because of the reliving of the past in what is known as the analytical transference. The dread was no picnic, linked with the childhood fear of returning home and finding mother drunk.

The longing arose from the dependency and acute need for an adult who would be responsible for me. Of course no one ever could be. The damage done in childhood, if severe enough, is irreparable. But for a fortunate few, Freud's dictum that an ability to love and work is probably the most we can hope for, and the gradual replacement of neuroticism with genuine loneliness and sadness is progress indeed, and I started confiding my dreams, dilemmas at work, and the guilt I experienced, whether or not I was in the wrong. For example, I felt guilty if I spent money on myself and I bought a new winter coat identical to the one it replaced so that M.C. would not consider me extravagant. I told her this and she gave one of her rare laughs, but she remarked that money seemed to be one of the things I felt I could not control.

I had problems with all-pervasive guilt and although this diminished over time it remained a handicap. I ceased feeling guilty about the liaison with James. "But it was James who was committing adultery, not you" she said. Well, you could have fooled me, I did not comment.

I have always tended to feel responsible for everything and everybody (otherwise the world would fall apart?) and indeed my mother might have died if I had not been there; and perhaps if I had been more sensitive to my father's sadness he would not have killed himself? So I had good reason to watch over people. But M.C. put an end to my assumption that I was responsible for how other people chose to behave. When I told her I was embarrassed about a colleague who was rude to a waiter, "You feel responsible for how others behave?" And I realised that it was none of my business. Social workers are taught to be non judgmental, but it had not percolated into my private life.

My mental confusion as an adult did not come from being unloved as a child but from being grossly neglected and frightened. With M.C. I sometimes re-experienced these encapsulated terrors. Travelling in the tube one evening on my way to her I read of some atrocity to a child inflicted by a psychopathic parent, and I arrived for my session paralysed with terror. Mother's perverse sexual fantasies had made a terrible imprint and reading about the atrocity left me floundering in helpless disgust. That evening we went on to talk about my mother's other distorted projections, including her accusations that I was lesbian, which, although I later appreciated had some basis in reality, as a child filled me with nameless dread and cast a shadow over all my friendships.

I trust M.C. implicitly but there came a time when I must have thought she needed sustaining, so I took her a present of a pound of smoked salmon. She looked slightly taken aback for a second, then must have accepted, realising that even the best mother cats get hungry at times with demanding kittens, but she made no facile interpretation. I just thought I was giving her a treat, and only later saw the symbolism.

Sometimes, when I was less depressed, I became very frustrated by M.C.'s perceived failure to be the responsive, 'ordinary mother' I wanted, and I once threw an ashtray in her direction. In a second she was at my side, leading me to the couch and covering me with a blanket until the storm passed. There were no other indications of the anger that must lie too deep in my psyche to be safely exposed.

I was not in treatment long before the first Easter break. M.C. did not think it safe for me to be at home without sessions with her for a week, knowing that I might commit suicide, and so she arranged for me to go into a nursing home, by some weird coincidence in Pinner. This was not chosen deliberately, but because M.C. knew the place personally. I said "But I can't leave Simon." "Of course not" she said, "he is going with you." I guess that the home was used to accommodating eccentrics, and Simon and I were made welcome and left in peace with books and music in a comfortable room overlooking gardens. The chef came up to take our order for dinner, and in due course brought our meal including a liver casserole for Simon who accepted everything with his usual trust, even allowing me to walk him in the garden with a harness and lead.

Gradually over the years my depression left me, leaving in its place sad loneliness. A successful analysis replaces neurosis with normal unhappiness. It certainly does not solve life's problems. I was functioning well at work and attending courses in psychiatry and developing my professional career, but away from work I was lonely. I had friends, but none were intimate. I began to think I would like a woman partner. The change from wanting, or drifting into bed with men may have come about as analysis exposed the sham of my liaison with James, and uncovered my essential sexuality which is bi-sexual, with a preference for sexual relationships with women.

It is difficult, in the 1990's, to recall the days when being gay or lesbian was deeply shameful, and, in fact, I never came out openly, marked as I was with some of the prejudices of my generation. But I thought about women, and spent summer days by the women's pool in Highgate, hoping I suppose that someone would approach me; but I did not know the signals to give, and I have the disadvantage of looking far too respectable, 'too good to be true' as someone once unkindly remarked. I heard about an underground lesbian club in Chelsea, in the Kings Road, and went to investigate. I was amazed to find myself in the midst of women dancing or sitting around drinking, smoking and petting. I cannot imagine what I expected, but I was happy to be in such a congenial atmosphere, although I lacked the experience which would have enabled me to feel quite at home. I could not have wanted to be, as I never repeated the experience. But on that night I approached a young woman drinking at the bar and offered her a drink. She was an American student and this was her first night in London. We went home together, my one and only one night stand with a woman.

I do not know if this is due to repression or caution, and perhaps a wish to stay in what is still felt to be the mainstream of society, though happily changing very rapidly. Analysis continued to be central to my life, and I began to talk about my father. M.C. wondered why such a conscientious man, about whom the coroner had written "Cecil Court left his affairs in perfect order", had failed to make provision for Peter and me. I began to wonder too, and went to Somerset House to get a copy of his will and found that he had left his estate in trust to his father "to be used at your total discretion for the benefit of my infant children." Peter and I never received a penny from the estate, or indeed any indication of interest from our paternal grandparents. When I told Peter, who was visiting London with his new wife, he was very angry, but we agreed it was not worth pursuing the matter. But it was good to know that our father had tried to take care of our future.

Peter had just completed an engineering contract in Argentina and came to England for two reasons, to look for further work in South America, contacting firms in London who employed British engineers, and also to sort out his divorce from Rhona, a childhood sweetheart, to legitimise his marriage to Grace.

I was unclear whether or not Peter had inadvertently contracted a bigamous marriage but I did not want him to have the bother of clarifying the situation to me, and perhaps causing him embarrassment. I went to Court with him and during the proceedings became none the wiser. But I understood that Peter must have been guilty of some misdemeanour when Judge Mishkin said sternly, "Do you think, Mr Court, that your behaviour has been that of an officer and a gentleman?" It was all I could do not to be convulsed with laughter and I distracted myself by thinking what a lovely name Mishkin would be for a cat, a tabby with a white ruff and dignified demeanour.

Grace and I went shopping to celebrate the end of the case and she told me of her concern for Peter who sometimes had panic attacks as well as asthma, and had "odd habits… He hides his dirty clothes at the back of the cupboard and he seems afraid to tell me if he breaks something accidentally. It's as if he is terrified of getting a scolding." She knew nothing about his childhood and I said I would ask him if he could share some of this with her which would help her to understand him better.

But it transpired that Peter remembered next to nothing about our early trauma, other than that mother drank to excess. Walking down Marylebone Road, past the hotel where our father had killed himself, Peter had a panic attack, gasping and clutching his heart. We sat on the steps of the library until he recovered. Looking away from me, Peter said, "But what happened to us as children? Every time I come to London I get ill, I can't breathe in this country." That evening in the flat he had rented, while Grace got us a meal, I told him gently that he had been cruelly treated as a child, and that this had left him frightened because he had buried the memory, and it only surfaced when he was in the place where it all happened. I did not tell him how angry I was that, because of this ill-treatment, he was never able to make his home in England, but had to be in permanent exile. He agreed to see a psychiatrist I recommended for some first aid for the panic attacks. He thought this would be a good idea, "I would do the same if my watch needed repairs" he said, "I guess I'm not ticking over the way I should."

Peter stayed in London long enough for a few psychiatric consultations at the Maudsley, and found a good job in Buenos Aires. We did not keep in touch as closely as I now wish we had, but his last years were happy. He embarked on a third marriage with a Spanish lady and found, in the end, domestic peace. His death from a heart attack in 1996 was unexpected. He was hard at work in his office when it struck, just giving him time to telephone his wife.

In 1963, Simon, now about fifteen years of age, began to show symptoms of kidney disease. He and M.C. were the anchors in my life and M.C. sustained me through the grief of his illness and death, as the time came when he could not even lap Brand's Essence. Seeing his distress one night, and not before time, I gave him a heavy dose of my own prescribed tranquillisers and he fell asleep and died peacefully in my arms. Since then I have had many cats, including Siamese, but in those days I did not have the resilience and capacity to bear grief as I do now.

I took an overdose the next week, waking up in hospital. I think this was a hysterical gesture, but it would have been fatal if M.C. had not telephoned the flat the next morning to see how I was, knowing that my first weekend without Simon would be desolate; and I was found unconscious.

I would never attempt suicide again, unless I had a painful terminal illness, because I felt such an extraordinary sense of wrong-doing as I swallowed the pills, one of the few religious experiences of my life.

It was not easy to say good-bye to M.C., internalised though she now was in my psyche, a source of inner strength and stability. For years, in dreams, I would seek a consultation with her when I was in conflict, and we did keep in touch for many years.

A few weeks later, a concerned friend said I should get another cat, "two preferably, for safety", and telephoned all the Siamese breeders he could find. As is often the case, there were no kittens available but eventually he tracked down two whose owners had to go unexpectedly abroad. M.C. did not think it a good idea to attempt to cut short the grieving time for Simon, but when Natasha and Pushkin arrived they did give me something to distract my mind, tidying up the books they flung from the book shelves and disentangling them from the curtains. At first I could not understand why I did not love them.

As the quality of my life improved, and the shadows of depression vanished, never to return in such a virulent form, old ambitions began to stir. I still wanted to get a degree, far from content with the diplomas I had although they were more than adequate for a social work career. Perhaps I knew too that I would find it impossible to break my dependence on M.C. without going away. In classical analysis you work towards a termination as part of the treatment in learning to deal with reality. But M.C., in her wisdom, chose not to, leaving it to me to say when I was ready to be on my own.

I talked about degree courses with my friends. There were still no undergraduate courses for social workers in the UK, and I sent for prospectuses from America. I had long been convinced that social work training in America was vastly superior to that available in the UK, being as here it was at post graduate level only. I chose to apply to Smith College, Massachusetts, an élitist college for women, that specialised in training social workers for psychodynamic clinical practice. My application for the shortened masters degree involved two summers on campus and a long winter placement in a clinical setting. I had enough money to pay for the course, but I obtained a Fulbright fellowship which covered the return air fare and health insurance. I arranged for two nurses to look after the cats and the flat in my absence.

Natasha and Pushkin were now little cats, although Pushkin remained small, the 'runt of the litter', but she was as brave as a lion. She would creep upstairs carrying a large sponge in front of her, so that all that you could see was this large object approaching with a long tail at the end. Apart from the year and a half I was in America, Pushkin was my little companion for seventeen years, surviving her sister Natasha by ten years, moving with me for her last ten years to Cambridge in 1977 to purr her way into a new life.

When the day came to leave London I was so terrified of setting out to fulfil my long cherished ambition to get a proper education, i.e. a degree, that my knees shook so much I could not get into the taxi, and laughing hysterically, my friend had to haul me in and we set off for the airport.

CHAPTER TWENTY FIVE

SMITH COLLEGE

1966-1967

I arrived in Boston in the blazing June heat, so what with that combined with travel exhaustion and anxiety, I had a mind-blocking migraine by the time I arrived in Northampton. I was late. I should in fact have arrived the previous day and when I presented myself to register for the course, student briefing sessions were in full swing. Helen Pincus, deputy Dean said "You wouldn't be able to take anything in anyway" and took me over to the student residence known at that time as a dormitory, where the twenty or so senior graduate students were housed in single study bedrooms. My room overlooked a beautiful quadrangle, tree-enclosed, and a green lawn. This was part of the 125 acre grounds developed by generations of benefactors to create one glorious garden of Eden; the whole campus an arboretum of massive trees, flowering shrubs, rose gardens, and specialist botanical areas with plants and seeds sent from all over the world and from the Royal Botanical Gardens at Kew and Java.

From the time the College was established in 1875, as a liberal arts college to further the education of women, dedicated gardeners, landscape designers and architects worked together to create an integrated lovely place where women could study in peace. By the mid sixties both men and women were admitted to the graduate school and there was one young man in our year.

Smith College is in Western Massachusetts in the Connecticut River Valley, close to Northampton, once an old mill town but now, judging from the description on the internet, it is yet another theme park. It was not when I was there. I am fortunate in that I have been able to work and study in so many unspoiled places, before they were ruined by so called development and their souls destroyed by tourism. But on this beautiful campus the green lawns still slope down to the aptly named Paradise Lake, with its romantic woods leading to the wild-flower strewn waterside foot paths, and slow rowing boats glide by with the wild fowl as if suspended in time in another dimension.

I wandered out to explore, helping myself to a peach from the dining room sideboard to feed to the first squirrel I met. He sat near me, turning the fruit over and over in his tiny paws. There was no one about that first evening. Staff and students were all being inaugurated in the class rooms; we would meet for supper later. I found Burton Lawn with its long swing immortalised by Elizabeth Taylor and Richard Burton early in the sixties in the film "Who's Afraid of Virginia Woolf?" Flying through the air I felt like a young girl, not a woman in her mid forties embarking on yet another serious voyage of discovery.

In England I had not really done much homework about Smith College, choosing it because of its specialisation in clinical social work and psychodynamic orientation, and because the forms they sent were easy to complete. I knew it was a private college but I had not realised how richly endowed it was financially, élitist and privileged. It just happens, I suppose, that I gravitate towards the best....from St Thomas Hospital onwards to prestigious Smith. Swinging into the future I was supremely happy.

I walked through the rose gardens to the Neilson Library. I knew it housed over a million books, Sylvia Platt's original manuscripts, and a huge repository of women's history manuscripts. I envisaged hours of peaceful reading and research, little knowing that the course would be so intensive and absorbing that there would be little time for reading beyond that demanded in assigned study over the next fifteen months.

I met my fellow students at supper. We sat formally round six to a table with one person assigned to carve. I was excused this task as a vegetarian. The dining rooms and sitting rooms were quite luxuriously furnished and I soon perceived that, although Smith students were indoctrinated with the Puritan work ethic, we were not required to be ascetic.

The senior students seemed a nice lot. Several were mothers with teenage undergraduate children whose husbands and children visited at the weekend to give mother a hand with her essays and help her change her typewriter ribbon. But no men were allowed to visit bedrooms, not even husbands, let alone cats. Over the next weeks I had quite a job smuggling Timothy, the black campus cat, into my room for his supper, and if the housekeeper came up I would deposit him in the clothes closet, a large wardrobe where I made up his emergency bed for such occasions.

There was no time wasted on our eight-week summer terms. Lectures began at 8.30am and every hour of the day was carefully scheduled, with the evenings free to write essays. We had all brought our own manual typewriters which clacked on into the night.

Fortunately for me, as expected, a good deal of the course content was familiar, and we were well taught by the resident academic and visiting staff, all of whom put the students' education first in their priorities.

Psychiatry, in particular, was brilliantly taught by Professor Howard Polsky who sometimes flew onto the campus from Boston and we prayed that his plane would not crash into the drink with our essays and exam papers. One of his lectures was on "the interplay of psychiatric factors and social reality." "This is what our clients have a lot of" I pencilled in my note book, thinking of the impact of poverty, deprivation and powerlessness affecting families throughout the world, including America. Professor Polsky gave due weight to all this and I noted "He's great fun, not a Smithy type at all, more of a protesting hippy." My perceived 'Smithys', like True Nightingales at St Thomas, tended to be earnest, establishment types, targets of my ribald iconoclasm.

Smith was quite conservative in the mid 60's but it has moved with the times, and now has full student participation – a commitment to encourage "students of colour" and an acceptance and welcome for gay students. Even in the sixties I was told that Smith had a name for being a 'hot bed of lesbianism' but this was not apparent to me. Most young students fraternised with men at Harvard and the local Massachusetts colleges at Amherst, Mount Holyoke and Hampshire.

We were soon immersed in the course, which included group theory, an area of study new to me, taught by Rachel, an associate professor of research. She joined us for supper the first evening after her session. Some of us who had not written research papers before were puzzled by the intricacies of foot notes and references and she quickly put our anxieties to rest with clear explanations and a simple written guide. She was about my age, dark haired, brown eyed, compactly built, quick in her movements and alert in responding to each of us. I thought her very kind and perceptive.

By now I had started to overcome my inhibition about taking part in class discussions and seminars, having discovered that assessments took this into account, and I was determined to get good grades. I also had a crazy idea that I should demonstrate the academic ability of British students (such patriotism!). I knew that the British were, on the whole, thought to be a lazy lot who lived off the welfare state. But I did not fully overcome my phobia about public speaking until several years later when, as an officer in the NSPCC, I was required to give talks to volunteer groups and speak to the media.

It was at Smith that my innate competitiveness and the desire to be a success really came out. Americans believe that anyone who works hard can succeed, and accolades and popularity follow in the train of success. No one pretends (as we do in the UK) that it's cool to be getting by with very little work, or attempt to hide the fact that achievement matters. But I was determined, not only to get 'A' grades, but to do better than all my fellow students. This neurotic ambition (so unBritish) was assisted by the nature of our studies, which were in the jargon 'ego syntonic', meaning that the material was in accord with what I really believed and or had experienced.

The 'Block' system at Smith, not unlike the modular system now in vogue in the UK, meant that we had exams at the end of each academic course in addition to the case work analysis and general essays. I would collect the marked papers with a casual air then, like a squirrel, take them to a quiet spot by the lake to devour, stopping on the way to dash into the loo so I could make sure I had an 'A' and to glance at the comments. Although I expected to do well, it continued to be a great joy to me when I did. It was hard to believe it really happened. The intense concentration and the high quality of the teaching, all in such a rarefied atmosphere, suited me well.

We had very little time for other than assigned reading but when we were asked to write a research proposal I wanted to do something different. Remembering India and the streets of Calcutta, I looked through medical journals in the Neilson library and designed a research project on 'Suicide in Calcutta' to examine the health and social factors leading to suicide amongst young brides. More joy when my effort was chosen to illustrate how such a project could be formulated. But all was not rosy. When it came to data analysis and statistics I was completely lost, and I only just managed to scrape through. I sometimes wonder if the stumbling block is my total lack of mathematics or a difficulty in logical thinking, or both.

The first summer term came to an end. We had a few days off and we were in turn summoned to our tutors for assessments. My tutor seemed to me to be neutral, quite pleasant but she made no comment about my excellent grades and I, of course, was expecting praise and recognition. I left her study very forlorn, and suddenly and alarmingly my psychic world slipped, and I was alone in the dark forest of desolation. I went to my room, unsure what to do, then remembering Margaret Collins, my analyst, I gathered up change, worked out the time scale, and rang her. I guessed that she would have seen her last client and be there for me, and so she was. Her voice alone was enough to restore the world's balance. It did not really matter what we said and I did not need to tell her what was wrong.

I met my tutor walking over to supper and now, back in my right mind, I told her that I had been troubled but that I was OK now that I had telephoned my analyst. She was quite shocked, "but you should have said you wanted to speak to your analyst and telephoned her from my room", and she went on to say that she had not praised my work because she assumed I was satisfied with my grades and she did not want to appear patronising, "more fool me" she added, "I should know better" and took my arm as we walked into the dining room.

Social workers and others often describe someone as vulnerable but most of us, if vulnerable at all, are only weak in patches, then "the crack in the teacup opens a lane to the land of the dead" as Auden wrote. Those who live on the verge do not go to pieces unless the flaw is touched. It's as well to know where the flaws are, although this does not prevent one becoming cracked under adverse circumstances.

All went well during the second term that summer. I enjoyed the company of my fellow students and at weekends we took picnics by the lake or walked to Northampton to buy books, drink coffee and play the juke box.

We were all getting anxious about our winter placements. I hoped, and requested that I go to Boston so I could explore that wonderful city, drift round the Harvard campus, sit by the river and trace the haunts of Henry James. But, alas, it was not to be. I was to go to Springfield, to the District Mental Health Clinic. Perhaps it was thought I needed an internship in adult mental illness rather than more experience in child guidance, and because the senior psychiatric social worker there was renowned for her skill with students from abroad.

My thesis advisor was to be Professor Roger Miller, the head of the research faculty. I guess I was given this honour because of the 'halo effect' of my 'A' grades, but from my first encounter with him, I felt a deathly chill, as if I had glided in a small canoe alongside an iceberg. Professor Miller, brilliant theorist, suggested I might like to look at "intuitive case work to see how the practitioner reaches decisions about a client's needs based on an intuitive understanding. You had a Jungian analysis" he said, "you could perhaps link up Jungian psychology in such a study." But I sat silent and frozen. Poor Roger Miller, a logical thinker if ever there was one, must have found me hard going.

It was sad leaving the beautiful campus, and I did not like the thought of eight months in a small American city, as it then was, but I found lodgings in a shared house not too far from the clinic and met the staff who were friendly and welcoming. I quickly settled into the work. Most of our patients were self-referred and fee paying, others were 'on welfare' and their fees reimbursed. We worked as a team led by an urbane excellent psychiatrist, Dr Robert Harrington, renowned for his knock-out 'half and half' gin and tonics as I discovered when I was invited to his home for a meal. My supervisor, Anne Connor, was helpful and encouraging and I would have felt quite relaxed if it was not for the vague cloud overhanging the thesis project.

Many of our patients were quite seriously ill, usually with depression, and after they had seen Dr Harrington and perhaps been prescribed medication, they were referred back to the psychiatric social workers for supportive therapy. It was not long before Dr Harrington noticed that I had acquired a heavy case-load of such patients, and said "enough of depressives, Joan, you have to take care, it's catching, I'd like you to take a few short term referrals of a less draining nature." And so I was referred a poor lady whose head had got fixed so that it was leaning on her shoulder following an occasion when she was looking in the mirror and saw a reflection out of the corner of her eye of her husband kissing the baby sitter. Weeping and angry, she was, after a few weeks, able as it were to face the facts and confront her erring husband. As so many situations are without remedy it is encouraging when things go well.

On another occasion a pale middle aged army officer referred himself and sat anguished and silent before blurting out "I feel sexually attracted by my daughter, you'll have to get me put away somewhere, I shall have to resign my Commission, I'm so ashamed." He wept. I spent some time with him and then arranged a joint interview with Dr Harrington as I thought he needed male reassurance. "Is it really true then that it is not unusual for fathers to have these feelings, so it's all in my head?" By then we were sure that no incestuous act had taken place and Dr Harrington had given some practical advice about avoiding the occasions of temptation and restoring the normal generation boundaries. We had three more weekly sessions to diffuse his anxiety and to help restore his confidence.

Meanwhile my own confidence was steadily crumbling in regard to the thesis dilemma. I had several supervisory sessions with Dr Miller but we made no headway, he could have been a stranger speaking in an unknown tongue for all I understood. It was a total derailment of any possibility of rapport or dialogue. I could not think, my mind was frozen. Returning back to Springfield in the Greyhound bus from what was to be our last session I wept silently as the cold night and the bitter rain swept down. In the bus station I tried to think what to do, playing 'Born Free' repeatedly on the little jukebox by the table, as if the memory of Elsa the lion would warm me up. Back in my lodgings I buried myself in space fiction in the other world of Arthur Clarke. I had never read space fiction before, but the occasion demanded an escape route to outer space.

My clinic supervisor encouraged me not give up but I knew that I had reached an impossible glacier and that I would have to retreat. The task, or the way it was presented, was not within my competence. So I wrote to the Dean expressing regret that "I am unfortunately unable to benefit from Dr Miller's supervision and begin working on a thesis", and that I would like to finish the course if I might, although "I realise I will not be able to graduate in the circumstances."

At Smith College it was unheard of to change thesis supervisor so I was astonished to have an immediate response from Dr Miller expressing regret that we could not work together and that Rachel, the associate professor I had met and liked on my first evening, had suggested to the research committee that she should meet with me to discuss arrangements about my thesis, and that I should contact her.

I telephoned her and we met in her office the same week. "I'm just going back for lunch" she said, "we could talk more comfortably at home if you would like to come and bring the coffee with you." Her car was parked by the research building, the ash trays full of cigarette stubs and the back seat covered in files. With coffee swirling in the precariously balanced mugs we headed for Rachel's home, where she lived with her friend and colleague Helen, a few miles from Smith College. In the car I was very conscious of Rachel's physical presence and her beautiful voice. She once remarked that she thought I listened more to the tone of a voice than to what was being said, just as young children do.

Helen, a large, warm hearted woman, lived and worked with Rachel for many years, not in a lesbian relationship but one founded on mutual professional interests. They wrote erudite social work books and papers together. I grew to understand that Helen gave Rachel a supportive domestic background which was always there like a family, but from which Rachel could sally out on her emotional adventures in freedom.

After lunch Rachel said "we'll deal with your thesis after tea; I have some suggestions you may like to consider but now we could sing. I hope you can sing?" Helen played the piano and we part sang old folk songs and as a kindness to me, a little ditty,

> "I've been to London, I've been to Dover,
> "I've travelled the whole wide world over."

Very appropriate to my past and indeed the future when I would make many harrowing journeys to Dover trailing the live export death trucks and their cargo of little lambs and calves.

On that long afternoon all I was conscious of was a feeling of dizzy exhilaration and relief. The icebergs had long since floated back to the Arctic.

We had tea and Helen went to her study to correct papers. Rachel put some Chopin on the record player and told me that she had looked at a trial research paper I had submitted the previous term about the institutionalisation of childbirth. "You could develop that theme" she said, her dark head bent over a folder. "I've done an outline for you, and a draft synopsis, in which, strange as it may appear to you, you summarise what you are going to research before you do it. You could start the first chapter with a historical review. You'll enjoy doing the library search. You will have to do that in the campus library. You could come over from Springfield for the day and use this house as a base if you like. Would you like a gin and tonic?", and taking our glasses we walked into the garden.

Fired up, secure, heart warmed so that my brain worked again, I returned to Springfield and began work on the thesis. I would have liked to illustrate it with interviews with women, to obtain their first hand accounts of hospital deliveries, but there was no time. I was very much behind with the schedule imposed by Smith College.

My interest in childbirth and my experiences as a midwife became known to women's groups in Springfield and I was asked to talk to groups who were seeking radical changes in hospital procedures. As a start they wanted their husbands to be allowed into the labour room to give support, and to enable them to hold the baby when it was born. I suggested that the couple chain or handcuff themselves together when labour began, and at the same time make sure the local paper knew about it. I was not able to take part in this exercise but apparently it succeeded in changing some of the more rigid obstetric regulations.

All this helped in writing the thesis, no longer a nightmare. So much of my former career as a nurse midwife, and involvement in the radical movement locally, gave life to the project. And there was Rachel to guide me through concepts and theories. I saw her regularly and on each occasion she would have read my draft work carefully and made suggestions and amendments. It must be said that she re-wrote a great deal of it, somewhat beyond the call of duty perhaps, but I was only too thankful. She invited me home so that I could make faster progress using her electric typewriter. Rachel was renowned for her generosity towards students and her creative teaching. It was not surprising that I fell in love with her.

Although I did not give the matter any conscious thought, I must have assumed she was a lesbian, or I would not have dared to say, as I got into her car one evening, "I know why I sometimes find it difficult to talk to you - it's because I love you". A statement that did not seem to surprise her unduly. She smiled "In that case I suggest we go into town for a celebratory coffee." And so it all began.

Although we were the same age, Rachel was much more sexually sophisticated than I and less overwhelmed with passion and desire, but she did respond to my love with great tenderness and to my inexperience with gentle amusement. This may have irked her at times but I had the attraction of being different, British, a cultural enigma. Whatever it was, the attraction was mutual and for me, sexually, it was sheer rapture.

One of the joys of love affairs between women is that it is easy to have orgasms and you do not have to bother with birth control. The physical intimacy between Rachel and me was of such intensity I felt I was using up a great sea of unfulfilled desire and at the same time storing up the beauty of it all for the future, when I might no longer be in her protective arms. "Do not expect again the Phoenix hour." I could not bear to think of the future, as the time in Springfield drew to an end and I returned to campus for the last eight-week term. The work pressure was immense and I had some difficulty balancing academic demands with the hectic secret life with Rachel. Secret, in the sense that no one spoke of our affair openly, although I knew it was a source of amused scandal on the campus. Rachel was asked by the Dean not to take students to her home, I believe, but as she had a room to sleep in on campus our nights together continued. The secrecy and the incestuous overtones of an affair between a member of the faculty and a student no doubt added to the intensity of my feelings.

I continued to work hard and with my thesis completed I handed the bound copy in on the appointed day. No extension of time was ever granted at Smith except in the case of serious illness. At least, in America, students know what is expected of them, a rigid structure that has its advantages.

All that was left to do now was to sit our exams and to present an outline of our thesis to faculty and students. This was an ordeal for which I prepared by taking a strong enough dose of valium to ensure composure without rendering me speechless. The session was chaired by kind, perceptive Helen, who enabled each student to feel encouraged and confident.

The magic summer came to an end. We graduated, celebrated and began our fond farewells to each other. Most of the American students would go home. I planned a brief stay in New York with Elmina Lucke, my social work friend from Karachi days.

I thought about staying in America, but I think it would have posed difficulties in relation to the terms of my Fulbright fellowship which was granted with the condition that recipients return to their own country to work, and my passage was booked on the Queen Mary. The degree itself had cost me about three thousand dollars in fees and board and I needed to get a job. Rachel and I talked about making our life together but I knew in my heart that this was not on. Perhaps it would have been better to have ended our affair then, but we were still in love and severance would have been very hard and I am not good at making tidy endings, preferring perhaps to hang on, hoping, often without grounds, in optimism that things will work out.

We said good-bye. She gave me an envelope which she said contained a letter for every day I was at sea. In my cabin I found a huge bunch of 'birds of paradise' flowers and on 6 September 1967 I sailed back to England. The prospect did not excite me, except I looked forward to being reunited with my little cats. I felt as if I had left half my soul behind. It was hard to return to the reality of everyday living. Even without the love affair with Rachel, the intensity of life on that heartbreaking, beautiful campus, left an indelible imprint, as it has on many lives.

Joan's group. Smith College, Massachusetts

Graduation. Smith College, Massachusetts

CHAPTER TWENTY SIX

NSPCC

1968 - 1971

I was welcomed back to my little top storey flat in Grove Terrace, opposite Parliament Hill Fields, by my landlady and friend Olive St Barbe, now rather frail and beginning to be forgetful, but still able to live independently. I was united with Natasha and Pushkin, the Siamese cats who looked at me blankly, unforgiving after such a long absence. They took a little time to respond, but when they did we curled up to sleep.

The grey English damp autumn closed in. I wrote to Rachel and bought a tape recorder so we could exchange tapes and I lived for her letters and her voice on the telephone.

Catching up with friends I began looking for a job. This was not difficult in the late sixties – there were plenty of jobs for social workers and with a Smith College degree I could have embarked on an academic career. I was invited to apply for a lectureship in a department of social work in a Midland university. I looked around the bleak campus, but still mesmerised by the eternal light of the Massachusetts sun and overwhelming nostalgia I did not apply for the job. I had also found out that the county was 'renowned' for fox hunting and that put me off. It would be fifteen years before the cause of animal rights became central to my life, but I knew enough to be aware of the cruelty of blood sports. I did not think of myself as a political activist in those days but looking back now it is apparent I was always a radical, and in the sixties I campaigned for the abolition of hanging, encouraged by the local MP who said "We will see an end to this obscenity" and so we did.

I found a job quite quickly in a small family case-work agency where I knew the standards were high, and that it would be possible to do good case-work. I stayed in this quiet backwater for several months, but I was restless for a more challenging opportunity, and responded quickly when the NSPCC advertised for a team leader to pioneer research and treatment of the battered baby syndrome. My friend Wendy, from Bristol days, said encouragingly "Put away those dusty files and go and make your name", and attracted by the chance to work on the frontier of new knowledge with mothers and babies in crisis, I applied for the job. I was accepted and the NSPCC director gave me a free hand to recruit a team and to develop the project as I thought best. I may not always have been wise in my choice of social workers for the team but I had an unexpected blessing when Ruby, a friend from Calcutta, now in London and looking for work as a secretary, agreed to join us and stayed as my personal assistant through the next three turbulent years, forging a link with the past, with Asia, my dreamland.

In 1967 my team and I certainly had an open field to investigate. There was very little literature about the dreadfully named 'battered baby syndrome', later to be amended to 'battered child', and then to 'non-accidental injury' and to take its place with other forms of child abuse and neglect. I found that there were only three or four articles on the subject dating from 1946. The first described the puzzling association between multiple fractures in the long bones of babies with chronic brain haemorrhage; ten years later a further article stated that these injuries were due to violence. Another ten years went by before a paediatrician in Denver, Colorado, Henry Kempe, cast the subject into the open with his seminal article "The Battered Child Syndrome" and drew world attention to the gravity and extent of the problem. The NSPCC with its long experience in fighting against child cruelty invited the Denver team to London, and thus the idea of the NSPCC conducting its own research was born.

Reading the literature and the files held by the NSPCC it was clear to me that my first task ought to be to interview parents, particularly mothers, who had injured or feared they might injure their babies. An advertisement for volunteers to help me plan a therapeutic programme brought an interesting and wide response from women from diverse backgrounds anxious to be helpful and to share their terrible experiences. With the promise of confidentiality I interviewed extensively and the programme we eventually built into the project was influenced by the wise and sad advice I received from this source.

As it would be some time before we could set up our quarters, away from the central NSPCC offices, we used the opportunity to do a retrospective study of the NSPCC records and published the findings "78 Battered Babies" which, although rightly criticised for its lack of good scientific methodology, yet became the cornerstone of much subsequent work and advice to Government. We got it right, in fact, in spite of the work being scientifically flawed.

The next step was to talk to medical people and social workers in children's departments to make contacts, learn what we could, and to establish links for the future. There was so much interest in the subject and we received considerable encouragement to tackle a problem to which, for decades, professionals had, on the whole, turned a blind eye. The idea that parents could injure and sometimes kill their own children stirred up very uncomfortable feelings. This was long before the days of the 'discovery' of child sexual abuse; these horrors were yet to come, and did not manifest themselves during the time of our project.

We found a building to house "The Battered Child Research Department" in Ladbroke Grove and called it Denver House, to honour Henry Kempe and his team. It needed considerable work done on it before we could move in so I arranged to go on a study tour to America to visit Denver and other agencies dealing with child abuse. I stayed for three weeks and I was soon convinced that we should use the Denver model as our template with the emphasis on therapy and good social work and prevention. We were less concerned at that time with the environmental, political or criminal sides of the problem which later played a significant role in social services departments as they became, willy nilly, predominantly agents of social control.

In America, of course, I visited Rachel. We stayed at a Boston hotel, and I was conscious of a vague unease, knowing in my heart I think that Rachel's love for me was fading. It was not founded on much in the way of mutual interests and the novelty, at least for Rachel, was wearing off. But she welcomed my idea that we should have a holiday in Corfu in the Spring.

This turned out to be a disaster, quite comic in retrospect, although not at the time. A true romantic, I booked a cottage by the sea said to have belonged to Gerald Durrell. It sounded fine in the brochure but my heart sank when we arrived. It was very primitive, with a well for drinking-water with a broken bucket, hardly any furniture and a dirty gas cooker. Poor Rachel. So we hired a car and found better accommodation. It was clear that 'abroad' was not for her, and certainly not off the beaten track.

Rachel returned to America and for a time we continued to send each other tapes and love letters until a few months later she wrote to say that, although she could no longer love me, she wanted always to be my devoted friend and colleague. I did not reply, and threw my energy into work, giving myself no time to grieve. I never had another lesbian love affair, and indeed, apart from a few brief encounters, my sexual life came to an end.

I was fortunate in not being short of friends, and I was at the peak of my professional career; the beginning of nearly thirty years in child protection, so there was plenty of challenge in my life, as there always would be, but part of me had died, and I remained without a partner.

It is strange, but I did not consciously choose to become an expert in child protection. I prefer working with adults and I do not feel I have any gift or aptitude for working with children, at least not toddlers. I have no idea how to play with them and I often find them boring. My idea of hell would be to work in a day nursery. I am able to relate to older children and teenagers, perhaps because I treat them with respect. There is probably a difference between caring for and working for children, and I continued to battle for their right to protection.

My work with the NSPCC soon became renowned and we had visitors from all over the country and from abroad to share knowledge. We were much in demand to give public talks and media interviews, and it was then that I finally lost all fear of public speaking. The subject was so gripping and I enjoyed being at the centre of so much interest. Authors and playwrights visited the centre and helped to arouse public discussion. Tony Parker's play 'When the Bough Breaks' was discussed in the centre and the story was so spot-on that not for the first time, and I hope not for the last, the public's imagination and understanding were awakened through dramatisation of tragedy.

By the end of the year our project was well under way. We had good links with local hospitals, health centres and the children's departments and set up the first national index of battered babies(later to become 'At Risk Registers') and interdisciplinary committees. As the slow process of bureaucracy was established, as we gave advice to Government and wrote numerous articles, I became known as the queen of the Battered Babies, a strange way to make one's name.

All the cases referred to us by the hospitals were heart breaking, but in some cases there was a happy outcome, perhaps because we were involved from the very beginning and parents did not have time to build up barriers and fabricate stories to explain the infant's injuries. Some referrals were due to a misdiagnosis. On one occasion we were called to the hospital to see a year old baby with multiple bruises and strange circular marks down his spine which we first thought to be bites. The Chinese parents, without a word of English, sat forlornly by the cot. With an interpreter the mystery was solved. The marks were due to rather strenuous cupping, the parents' effort to reduce the child's fever. He made a full recovery and we were invited to his home for a delicious meal, "because of the comfort you gave us". Little did the poor souls know that we had suspected them of injuring their son.

My happiest memory of our visitors was when Dame Eileen Younghusband called round. She was famous as an international pioneer of social work, and as a magistrate and author, then aged about sixty, she became my most valued mentor over the next twenty years until her death in 1981. A magical person, intuitive, wise and decisive. As a young girl she broke away from the conventional life as a debutante when she discovered, through doing her voluntary work, the conditions under which poor people lived in Stepney and Bermondsey. In her latter years she was instrumental in reorganising the whole structure of social work training and practice. She spent her childhood in Kashmir where her father, Sir Francis Younghusband, was British Resident in Srinagar. I had read all his books, fascinated by the life of such a remarkable man, visionary, diplomat, intrepid explorer and mountain climber, famed for his travels across the Mongolian deserts and the Himalayas, and his epic journeys to Tibet. He reverenced nature and believed, as I do myself, in the interdependence of all life, and that the eternal spirit pervades all things.

Eileen's links with India wove into the pattern of my regard for her. At what turned out to be my last meal with her, I said I would like to meet her on the balcony of the Simla Residency when we were both spirits, to gaze at the high mountains together. She agreed, but said "you may have to wait a long time." Soon after this she was in a fatal car crash in America, leaving behind a legacy of accomplishments and the afterglow of the friendships which she had nurtured with such perceptive warmth and generosity.

On our project we tried not to get involved with the police and the courts. We thought that it was difficult, if not impossible, to combine therapeutic case work with the role of law enforcement, which parents could not fail to perceive as punitive. This view will sound strangely out of date, but it has some merit. This stance may have been the beginning of some stress and ill-feeling within the NSPCC as I did not think it right to prosecute parents except in exceptional circumstances. The hierarchy, and the director in particular, thought this was none of my business.

At the same time as this confrontation was building up, I was becoming uneasy about how we were going to write up the research, the old problem of my difficulty with concept models and data analysis. It was, though, time to consider getting on with this. Motivations are always very mixed. I wanted to challenge the Society, and I had a good reason to do so, but perhaps my eventual dismissal was in accord with an unconscious wish to get out.

Matters came to a head when the Society chose to prosecute a young single mother in the Isle of Wight, who took her baby to hospital with a minor injury. He was not admitted but was brought back a few weeks later with further injuries. The NSPCC chose to prosecute her and she received a heavy fine which she was in no position to pay. The poor woman said in her defence "I thought the hospital would admit him the first time", as of course they should have done. I chose to write a critical letter about this case to the director, incensed by the injustice.

Well, in those days, you would no more challenge the director than you would a charging rhinoceros, which in fact he closely resembled. Coincidentally, I had asked the organisation for a rise in salary for one of my team. This gave the NSPCC a reason to ask me to resign, saying I was dissatisfied with the terms of service. I refused, and next day I was told to leave the centre, my contract terminated. In those days there was no difficulty in firing workers, and the NSPCC had no trade union, though it was rightly suspected that I was urging officers to form one.

Although being dismissed was hardly a surprise it was, nevertheless, quite a shock. In these kinds of circumstances you quickly find out who your friends are, and I was not really surprised when I found my deputy reading letters sent to me and signing correspondence two days before I left. He couldn't wait to take over. But the administrative staff and friends outside were very loyal and supportive and gave me a farewell party. It had all happened so suddenly that I was dazed and wandered round London wondering what to do, until I remembered I must go home and feed the cats.

What happened after this did come as a complete surprise. An influential friend within the NSPCC headquarters notified the press and radio, and by the next day my spies informed me the director had to deal with a barrage of enquiries about why I had been fired. There were letters to The Times from eminent paediatricians and psychiatrists protesting at my dismissal, and it was said that there hadn't been a row like it since the end of the 19th century when two child protection agencies were at loggerheads. Petitions were signed demanding my reinstatement, and the press continued to harass the director. I began to feel better. It was rumoured that the director had been summoned by the Queen to explain the situation.

Left to my own devices I would have done nothing, except probably to mope and get depressed, as well I might, suddenly without the stimulation of an exciting job and being at the centre of a pioneering enterprise. As it was I received so much support, for which I shall always be grateful, especially to one or two senior social workers who telephoned every evening with helpful advice. I was also amused and touched by various friends who went on sabotaging the NSPCC's efforts to get me out of the system by setting up more media attention and bombarding headquarters with petitions. This experience taught me quite a lot about methods of campaigning.

In the years to come the NSPCC moved into the 20th century, formed excellent specialist units, remodelled their training and ensured that their officers became specialist social workers, thereby ending the days when they were perceived as the 'cruelty man' taking errant parents to court.

I was not reinstated, nor did I want to be, and after a time the rumpus died down and I began looking for work. There was no shortage of offers and I had to find a job soon to be able to keep my cats in the style of life to which they were accustomed.

CHAPTER TWENTY SEVEN

CIVIL SERVICE

1972-1977

It is a curiously unconnected feeling not going to work if you are accustomed to it. I had been working or studying since the age of twelve, so I felt like a sea anemone washed off a rock. My heart goes out to all those who are forced out of work in the brutal nineties. I had exhausted the possibility of work abroad in the third world, as it was then called, as I had educated myself out of further jobs with UNICEF or WHO by qualifying in social work, and my speciality in child protection rather than community work meant I was unskilled in potential openings in the Commonwealth Office. I would have been ambivalent about this in any case because I distrusted a paternalistic approach and interference with the culture of what were then thought to be backward nations needing enlightenment from the western development world. I felt critical of James, who had just completed an assignment on a Pacific island and produced a five year plan designed to create economic progress by motivating the inhabitants to move into unfamiliar markets with the island coconut and copra harvest. To do this meant that the people would have had to become competitive and 'aggressive' but the whole culture was interwoven with a code that was totally opposed to individualism, competition and a market economy. Their way of life was doomed but I recoiled from applying for any job which might hasten this progress so that when an opportunity occurred in Uganda I turned it down. "The villagers, where you would be working, still sleep on the mud floor of their huts" said my interviewer "your first task could be to get them onto beds." Back in 1971 it seemed that my karma did not include attempts to open new frontiers of knowledge and experience.

It was difficult to decide what to do next. Then an unexpected chance arose which was to enable me to consolidate my years with the NSPCC. A colleague urged me to apply for a vacancy in the Social Services Inspectorate of the Department of Health and Social Services. This was a central Government Civil Service job, and for the life of me I could see no possibility of anyone thinking I would fit into this massive bureaucracy, but it seemed worth a try.

The interview was intimidating, but although I had no hope or serious wish to succeed, I did my best to appear keen and intelligent to make up for being unable to give sensible answers to the questions posed. The urbane chairwoman, who looked like an upmarket edition of Betty Boothroyd, fielded me an easy opening at the end, perhaps despairing of getting me any marks at all, asking me my views about the role of voluntary agencies in the Community. It was clear to me that my chances of being recruited were nil as I knew that the civil service procedures for selecting candidates, particularly at this senior level, were based on scrupulous impartiality and objective marking. I would love to have seen the comments made by the selection board which resulted in my being appointed. It could only have been because of my knowledge of 'battered babies' and the pressure put on Government by the NSPCC to "do something" about it in the face of mounting public concern. "Well, you've got yourself a job for life" a friend remarked, "and in any case you'll have to stay for five years for a pension", knowing that I had made no financial provision for retirement.

As I had no intention of ever retiring, regarding it as the kiss of death, my first few months in the DHSS, housed at that time in the old Home Office building in Horseferry Road, were gloomy and dull, but I did my best to understand the system, the intricate grading of personnel, like cabbages, and the constant and understandable ambition and rivalry this engendered. Many years later, when Richard Adams, the genius who wrote 'Watership Down', came to talk to our animal rights group in Cambridge, he told me bitterly of his chagrin and anger at failing to gain the promotion in the Civil Service he believed he deserved, "then I write a stupid book about rabbits and suddenly I'm famous and rich. No, I don't want to see your rabbits, I can't stand them."

From the windows of my twelfth floor office in the monstrous sick building, Alexander Fleming House, where we moved at the end of the year, I looked out over the wilderness of the Elephant and Castle and the surrounding concrete blocks of the housing estates, already crumbling into decay and human misery, housing cooped up families seeking what escape they could in drugs and crime. Unlike the poor battery hens and factory pigs and calves they at least had opportunities to escape the reality of their hellish environment.

Feeding pigeons, strictly against office regulations, and sometimes getting a glorious sighting of a kestrel swooping above surveying the concrete cliffs for food and a nesting site, I enjoyed the company of Ivy, a Lambeth lady graded as a messenger, who endlessly pushed her trolleys of files up and down the gloomy corridors. Her little sorting room was an oasis, with shelves of beautifully tended African violets. We were discouraged from having plants in our offices, but the status of messengers in the civil service is so low that they may have been exempt from some of the regulations that ordered our lives. Regulations determined the size of the carpet in each officer's room, and I believe those who rose to astronomical senior heights had their own tea-sets. All this was a long way from the NSPCC Denver House where I had encouraged individualism to an extent that would have shattered the dusty windows of Alexander Fleming House. Our most efficient co-ordinator at that time liked to cook herself a kipper before starting work, and the team secretary worked with her new baby in his carry cot beside her desk. The latter, far from distracting people from their work, appeared to accelerate the pace by creating a loving ambience.

Although I was never exhilarated by the five years I spent in Government, I found it more interesting as I was allocated subjects to work on which I knew something about, "all connected with sex and/or violence" a colleague unkindly remarked, including family planning, unmarried mothers, as they were then called and later 'battered wives', whose existence was being exposed by a brave unconventional pioneer whom the Government wished, I am sure, would go away. Such campaigners are always vigorously resisted and it takes perseverance to break through the stone-walling of apathy and the constant discouragement of ministerial letters, all saying nothing at great length, drafted by the lower EO's (executive officers) and signed by an indifferent minister. Letters from MP's and individuals perceived as having influence in the affairs of state were responded to more cautiously. Battered wives ceased to be invisible because of the perseverance of a few individuals who would not give up as Margaret Mead rightly observed: "Never doubt that a small group of thoughtful, committed citizens can change the world: indeed, it's the only thing that ever does."

Other subjects came to me for comment, on which I was supposed to give advice or an opinion, including national emergencies such as the rising of the Thames and the arrival of refugees at Brize Norton. These matters involved giving advice to local authorities up to central government, and fortunately my part was not essential or London would have been flooded and refugees left stranded at the airport with me standing helplessly by.

The system in the department which ensured that the Minister, then Sir Keith Joseph, was properly briefed, required administrative civil servants to do the initial draft of whatever matters arose. This was then circulated by Ivy and her fellow messengers to the professional advisers, the social workers, doctors and nurses who made their comments, and then returned the file to the first scribe who would rewrite and finalise the briefing note. The speed at which this was done depended on the perceived urgency of the matter and the file was appropriately tagged. It took me a little time to work out which was most urgent, 'urgent' or 'immediate'.

Life became much more interesting when a new direct entry principal was appointed to my section, recruited from a university department of philosophy. We worked together on all the fatal cases of "battered babies", trying to analyse the files and content of public enquiries. His compassion and high intelligence made it easier to cope with this emotional barrage so that I was not overwhelmed with anger and distress as each sad story unfolded.

In my third year in the ministry a local authority asked if I could be permitted to act as an expert witness in the tragic death of Maria Colwell in Brighton, a little girl who was returned against her will to her mother from a loving foster home, and killed. Giving evidence in this case resulted in me being appointed in similar cases after I left the department and to continue work for children as the law changed to give them more protection, so that solicitors would present their case and an independent social worker safeguard their interests. One cannot say that these children did not die in vain, but their deaths did result in an upheaval in the law so that the rights of children were recognised, though with the inevitable backlash such progress arouses, such as opposition to the idea that parents should be prohibited from hitting their children, in line with the regulations which stopped corporal punishment in state schools and children's homes.

We worked hard in the department drafting memos and circulars and regulations concerning battered children (by then called 'non-accidental injury'), mostly based on the pioneering work of the NSPCC, which I found ironically amusing, even more so when the NSPCC director and his senior staff came to see Sir Keith Joseph to ask for a government grant and at the meeting I was asked for comments. The humour of the situation was not lost on Sir Keith, who was far from remote and always courteous to his advisers. I did, though, make my peace with the director, shaking his hand, marking, I think, the first time in history that a fired member of the NSPCC rose, as it were, from the outer darkness to effect a reconciliation.

The deaths of children were sometimes discussed in Parliament and we were occasionally required to attend Sir Keith in the House of Commons to give him a briefing note, hastily scribbled and passed to him by invisible sleight of hand.

On one occasion, late on a Friday evening in December 1973, the death of a little boy, Graham Bagnall, was debated in the House. There were fewer than half a dozen MP's present. Who cares? I thought angrily, haunted by the grim history of this child's death, and of the many others whose circumstances I had analysed and considered over the years, their suffering and loneliness so starkly described in the files.

Although I was interested in much of the work I was assigned, some of it I found tedious and fatiguing, particularly in committees, where I never felt I could contribute much, and I was often ill-prepared. Unless you are a barrister or a gifted high ranking civil servant it is difficult to absorb so much information at the speed required, certainly it was for me.

When the short debate finished, absorbed in thought I lost contact with my colleagues and wandered through corridors of the Houses of Parliament. At the best of times I have very little sense of direction, and clutching my permit and with an identifying label pinned to my coat, no one challenged me. I must have taken several wrong turnings and ended up at a door marked House of Lords Robing Room. I quickly looked for a messenger to guide me out, away from the sad ghost of Graham Bagnall.

CHAPTER 28
MARKING TIME

I felt I was marking time in the department but the daily tedium was enlivened when I was instructed to go as a delegate to a UN conference on the status of women and family planning, in Istanbul. It was wonderful to have the chance to wander through the covered markets and sail to the magic island on the Marmora sea, locked in a time warp woven in acacia trees, rickety wooden houses leaning across the narrow streets, birds flying in and out of the unshuttered windows, building their nests in dusty cupboards, and storks returning to make their homes on the roof: sacred birds protected by the army as harbingers of spring, and because they wintered near Mecca.

I flew out a few days before the conference to give time to explore the city, staying at the Bristoli Otel. Wandering out one evening a little tabby cat leapt out from a rubbish bag winding round my feet and demanding love and food. This posed a problem as it was late and it was not a shopping area. We wandered back to a better lit street and finding a night club persuaded the dazed door man to fetch some yoghurt and a lamb kebab.

Clutching these delicacies and the cat I returned to Otel Bristoli. I think the little cat may have been on heat as she sang and made nests in my arms all night.

Next morning I could not persuade the hotel to keep her, but they provided her with a nourishing breakfast, bread and butter, cheese, scrambled egg and milk. I had to leave for the conference and register at the delegates' hotel ready for work the next day, Monday. I walked up the road with the little cat purring on my shoulder and there, miraculously, stood the British Consulate set in a lovely garden. People were streaming in for the morning service. Assuming by their hats that the worshippers were mainly British I knew that little cat, with her winning ways, would wind herself into someone's home and heart, as she had demonstrated to me she had no hesitation about talking to strangers. Or perhaps she would choose to stay in the Consulate? I stayed for a time, until I heard the closing hymn then left her singing on the bench in the sun in the care of St Francis.

I enjoyed the conference and meeting the delegates from the newly emerging African states, and from Asia and Russia. Talking to the family planning experts from Pakistan it was good to hear how matters had gone since I left eighteen or so years before. I was told that I was regarded as their "martyr to the cause" and that birth control was now fully accepted by government. Back in the stultifying civil service I planned other ways of keeping my soul alive, and putting two lots of leave together I planned to go with a group overland to India and to meet Bela in Delhi.

In the mid seventies it was still possible to travel through Iran and Afghanistan and over the Khyber Pass to Pakistan and India. So this we did under remarkably primitive conditions using methods of transport which were dangerous, including travelling in overloaded trucks and worn out taxis through the Khyber Pass. "Do you ever give more than a passing thought to God?" an Indian fellow passenger asked as we rocked on, clinging to each other.

The highlight of this adventure for me was staying in Herat, in Afghanistan, with its ancient monuments erected in the time of Alexander the Great, now probably a heap of rubble since the Russian invasion. There were very few cars on the road but the traffic policemen were busy signalling the way to horse-drawn carriages, each horse brilliantly decorated with silver ornaments standing high between their ears, and scarlet pom-poms. I rode in one round the historic city and then explored on foot. Everywhere there were men polishing and cleaning their guns or crouched in doorways selling their wares including little moulds of opium and hashish. Judging by the far-away look in the eyes of many of the men there was a good market for drugs.

Walking down a narrow alley I heard horses neighing from an enclosed courtyard and stopped. A silver-bangled arm beckoned me in and the girl gestured for me to come upstairs. It emerged she was the town's midwife, and knew a few words of English. The room was taken up by a loom where a young girl ("new wife" my hostess explained) covered her hair and face and went on silently with her intricate weaving. We drank tea, ate little sugary cakes and communicated with gestures and smiles. When it was time for me to leave, my new friend placed a silver embossed ring on my wedding finger, my most treasured possession, and I gave her the Liberty scarf I was wearing. "That was a beautiful encounter" I said to the horses as I left, giving them a hug and adjusting their scarlet pom-poms.

We had all too little time in Herat, but the visit ended happily and appropriately in the circumstances. Late in the evening I finished packing and, wanting a cup of tea, walked up the road looking for a café. Hearing music and seeing a lighted room I walked in and found most of my fellow travellers sitting round drinking tea and smoking. I liked the smell of the smoke; "it's hash" one of the teachers explained quietly, perhaps suspecting, rightly, that it was new to me, and demonstrated the rituals that went with the experience. It gave me a wonderful feeling of relaxed intimacy and we talked quietly for what may have been many hours, or so it seemed to me. Back at the hotel I noticed that I was attempting to wash my face with the soap container and murmuring happily "you're stoned" I went to bed. I have never felt so relaxed before or since, as across my entranced mind wandered unicorns and white antelopes, elegantly streaming down on either side of a medieval hill. Next day I remarked to one of the teachers on the trip, "I can't think why you don't smoke that lovely stuff every day" and she replied, "but my dear girl, how would we ever get any teaching done if we did?" I suspect that the substance we smoked may have been laced with a little opium, or maybe it was just the best hashish – mind-enhancing whatever it was.

We arrived rather shaken in Rawalpindi. From there we crossed our last frontier into India, and then continued by train to Delhi. By then many of my companions were ill with diarrhoea, probably due to food poisoning from eating warmed up meat dishes on the Frontier. They lay on the luggage racks and on the floor and I did what I could for them until they could get proper care in Delhi.

In Delhi we parted sadly, our amazing adventures a common bond as, adjusting our rucksacks and our dishevelled selves, we hailed rickshaws and went our separate ways. Bela met me in the Hindu home where she had arranged we should stay. It was odd being in civilised surroundings again at the end of five weeks of gypsy life. Bela, my beloved Indian sister, did not look well, thinner, and she said she felt tired. I assumed that her lifetime working in the villages was taking its toll, but her fatigue was more likely to be due to early symptoms of the blood disorder which led to her death a decade later. Her white cells may have been killed by constant exposure to agrochemicals liberally sprayed on all crops by illiterate peasants unable to read the instructions on the product. These drained from the soil into the 'tanks', as village ponds were called, used by the villagers for all domestic purposes and as drinking water for animals. I mused bitterly that not only were millions of animals killed in pharmaceutical laboratories in appalling toxicity tests but countless more would be poisoned by the products exported to third world countries.

Back at my desk and renewed by this adventure I attempted, without much success, to immerse myself in work and it was then that a friend said "It's time you joined the middle classes and bought a house", an idea which had never occurred to me. It was not usual in the mid seventies for single women, let alone those in their fifties, to buy property. And who would give me a mortgage when I was likely to be without a job in less than four years? But there did not seem to be any difficulty about this – it was soon to be the time of the property boom, and the little terraced house I found in Wandsworth near the railway in a back street leading to Putney Bridge Road was not expensive.

I moved in with Natasha and Pushkin who at first did not seem too pleased with the small enclosed back garden, but they liked the extra house space and skidding across the wooden floor. I hastily built a raised flower bed in the garden against the factory wall at the end and made a lawn in a tin bath which Pushkin used as a sun bed, and I ordered an instant garden from an expensive garden shop in Chelsea: four large tubs resplendent with standard roses, petunias and lobelias. The roses smelled the enclosed stagnant air and promptly died but later other plants did well, fed by seasoned horse manure from the nearby Young's Brewery, and grew to amazing size.

I noticed that Natasha looked a bit off colour, her immaculate coat patchy, and she lost weight. The vet diagnosed feline leukaemia and I did not let her linger in misery. Little Pushkin, the runt of the litter who was never ill, pottered about saving her energy until a ripe old age. But she and I were lonely in a one-cat household and I contacted the Cats Protection League for a companion cat.

In the home there were many to choose from, but I was chosen by a large matronly tortoiseshell who extended a paw through the wire fence. I called her Suki Susanna but various visiting local children decided that as she had come from a home she should have lots of names to help build up her confidence, and she became Suki Susanna Victoria Puss-in-Boots Away-in-a-Manger Carpet Cat, the latter because she looked like an expensive oriental rug, and 'Away-in-a-Manger' the children said "because she had been in care." The children and I agreed that she need only use her full name on special occasions, "especially at Christmas."

At the Department we were becoming increasingly busy because new children's legislation was brewing, and we were consolidating guidance on child abuse for the local authorities and working out the role of the police in child protection cases. At the same time there was interest in researching what became known as The Cycle of Deprivation and parenting in general. I was asked to help plan an interdisciplinary conference on parenting to be held at All Souls in Oxford, and I suggested that we invite a social anthropologist, Dr Esther Goody from New Hall in Cambridge whom I had met and liked at various committees on family violence. She was unable to come, but Professor Mary Douglas from University College accepted the invitation. An august body of delegates assembled in the great conference hall in All Souls, senior civil servants, educationists, psychologists, psychiatrists, social workers and the Minister of Education, Margaret Thatcher. She was regarded as a bit of a tyrant and from time to time we were threatened with the possibility that she might swap ministries and come over to us. But it did not happen.

I thought Oxford was wonderful and between sessions ambled through the colleges, reading the notice boards and envying, in a vague way, the lucky students who could choose to go to such wonderful lectures. In sessions I made notes as each participant delivered an erudite paper, some of them bearing little relationship to life as I knew it. On the second day a senior civil servant came up to me to say "an old school friend of yours wants to meet you" and introduced Professor Mary Douglas, a grey haired, rather dumpy woman of my age, and so after four decades I met again Mary Tew of Totnes, my best friend from the convent in Torquay, and we had a tearful reunion in the cloakroom. Mary said that she had never had a best friend since we parted. Soon after I left school her own mother had died, at about the same time as my father, but her education went on conventional lines, and she had a distinguished career as a social anthropologist and married an academic conservative.

After the conference she gave me copies of her books. It was wonderful to meet my childhood friend again, but our lives and interests had developed along different lines, and politically we were miles apart. So our friendship did not take root again, but her books did and were to have a far reaching influence on my life.

CHAPTER TWENTY NINE

CAMBRIDGE

1977

I began to get quite worried about my future. At 57 I only had three years before compulsory retirement. I thought it likely I would continue to be asked to act as an expert witness in child abuse cases, and so it proved, but with only the small pension from the State and the DHSS I would not be able to pay the mortgage and keep my beloved pets in the comfortable style I thought they deserved, and I could see no way to fulfil my need for adventure and challenge.

The winter was dispiriting and gloomy as ever in grey London as I worked in the even greyer block at the Elephant and Castle, far removed, alas, from the natural habitat of the real beautiful, shadowy, elephants treading with silent feet along the dusty African roads.

I had two weeks leave due and I decided to go to St Lucia. The Caribbean was not my idea of adventure but there would be sun and blue skies and palm trees, the usual tourist dream I thought, folding my umbrella as I booked the trip.

I packed Mary Douglas's Penguin books 'Purity and Danger' and her essays on 'Implicit Meanings and Symbolism of Animals in Lele', more from a desire to understand my friend's life than from an expectation that I would find the books interesting. For good measure I thrust a selection of other anthropology classics among the summer dresses, 'Political systems of the Nuer', who were they? I wondered, and who or what were the Lele and Malinowski's classics on New Guinea 'natives'? Well, at least I knew where New Guinea was. I packed a good selection of novels and 'who dunnits' as an insurance if the text books proved to be as heavy going as I expected.

The tourist paradise of St Lucia was not surprisingly all that any sun starved Britisher could wish, and stretched out in the shade, complete with books, a rum drink and with the hypnotic steel band in the background, I leafed through the first chapter of 'Purity and Danger', and I was instantly transported into a new realm, gripped by my first immersion into the world of social anthropology. The drums beat in the background as I followed the Nuer and their tall antlered cattle to their winter grazing grounds, exchanged shells in the reciprocity elaborate *kula* rituals of the Trobriand islanders in New Guinea, and worked out the religious significance of the animals in the Lele tribes.

The scholarly work of intrepid researchers seeking to find the meaning and ritual significance of the ceremonies and the social structure in what were then called primitive cultures, and in the equally complex societies in the developed world, were a revelation to me, far removed from the cliché-ridden bureaucratic medical and social work professional books and journals I normally read.

These were not accounts of objective research and boring sociological analysis but highly theoretical concepts looking for patterns and meaning in the beliefs and cultures of the people among whom the anthropologist lived, sharing their lives. These concepts were not alien to me, as I remembered how I had encouraged my Punjabi and Bengali students to respect and study the culture and customs of their patients.

"Blast", I thought, "I'm in the wrong career, I should have been a social anthropologist", appreciating that such a career would have been immensely intellectually satisfying and given me all the adventure and the constant new frontiers my nature demanded, but ignoring the fact that had this been my fate I would have soon wanted to relieve the poverty and treat the disease-ridden tribes I was studying. But I always wanted to have the best of all possible worlds.

Packing up these entrancing books I felt that at least I now knew about Mary Douglas's world, thinking that my life as a social anthropologist would have to wait for another incarnation.

Back in London I hugged the cats, went back to work and accepted an invitation to have supper with an old friend, a psychotherapist, Joan Hunter, to catch up on our lives. Over our meal she asked "What next then for you, Joan?" "I wish I knew" I replied. "What would you do if you had a free choice?" "Why" I said, surprising myself "I'd be a social anthropologist" adding "preferably specialising in Shamanism so that I could learn how to cure people with ritual and ceremony." She smiled, "so you know what to do, as you always do."

Next day I telephoned Esther Goody in Cambridge, whom I had recently met again when she was advising about West African families and their difficulties in relation to fostering their children in white foster homes. I said I was thinking of changing my career and reading for a degree in social anthropology. "What a splendid idea", she said, "Can you come to lunch at New Hall on Friday?"

Over the meal "vegetarian over there" she said, she explained that the course would normally involve a three year undergraduate degree, but as I already had academic qualifications I might be accepted as an affiliated student, and so complete the course in two years. She must have thought that at my age I would prefer to take as short a time as possible. As it was I would be swapping my student concession card for a pensioner's rail ticket by the time I graduated. In retrospect I wish I had asked to do the full three years and thus have gained a knowledge of archaeology for free as there would have been an introduction to this in the first year.

I was very lucky to get admission in any case, as it was well past the regulation time for applicants for the 1977 academic year. Fortunately I was excused from taking an entrance examination, and my lunch with Esther Goody counted as an interview, to my surprise, and on 21 April 1977 I received the letter of acceptance from the Vice President of New Hall.

I went round in a dream, walking on air as I solemnly dealt with my in-tray, as ever casting my own romantic imaginative net over Cambridge, Mecca indeed for a woman who struggled fifty years ago to take the matriculation exams through the Wolsey Hall correspondence course. I was soon to matriculate by signing a form in New Hall. I re-read all the classic novels and essays about Cambridge, Virginia Woolf and E M Forster and also studied the reading list from New Hall, which was enough to throw me into a turmoil as I began to appreciate the intellectual challenge I had let myself into: theories about lineage, economic and political structures, religion and caste (that would be all right) symbolism and ritual, way beyond my intellectual grasp I thought, but I knew enough not to be deterred by reading lists and went ahead applying for a grant. In those days students eligible for a major award for a first degree got one automatically, but my application to the Department of Education put them in a spin, as I already had an MA and the Civil Service found it hard to deal with such an upside down request. But it all worked out in the end. All that remained to be done in the next four months was to arrange to sub-let my house and to find lodgings in Cambridge. I intended to continue in gainful employment until the week before term began.

Dame Eileen, with whom I went to have tea and to tell about my plans, was encouraging, "then all you will have to do when you graduate is to find a tribe in India and live with them for a couple of years, that shouldn't be difficult." She added, smiling benignly, "you probably have at least another good ten years of working life ahead of you."

I pondered about all this as I sat on a bench at the entrance of the Arndale Centre in Wandsworth, one of the first of the monstrous shopping arcades soon to destroy every city. Out of the corner of my eye I noticed a little scrabbling in the shrubs of the small raised flower bed nearby. Careful not to attract the attention of any passer-by who might harm them I fed the mouse family my sandwich and then went into the Arndale Centre to buy grain and to pick up a plastic cup of water from MacDonalds, cut to size, explaining "my little dog" was thirsty. "Will they survive, I wonder, and be able to raise mouse families in the concrete jungle? Will any of us?"

It's all very well for me , I thought soberly, being able to look forward to a whole new life. But what of the animals, our fellow creatures on this doomed planet? My physicist friend, whom I met from time to time, tried to reassure me, "Nature always triumphs in the end" he said.

I find it hard to be optimistic but this will not, I hope, prevent me from continuing to fight for mice and for human beings in distress, and I am comforted, as ever, by the patter of little feet as my aged cats, well beyond the age of hunting, struggle onto my lap and desk to give what assistance they can in the struggle. "You have to keep on purring, it's the only way to survive."